Access your online resources

SEND Leadership is accompanied by a number of printable online materials, designed to ensure this resource best supports your professional needs.

Go to https://resourcecentre.routledge.com/speechmark and click on the cover of this book.

Answer the question prompt using your copy of the book to gain access to the online content.

SEND Leadership

SEND Leadership completes the Essential SENCO Toolkit trilogy and provides SENCOs and SEN Practitioners with the guidance and tools needed to aid their leadership and quality assurance (QA) roles.

The book explores the intent, implementation and impact of SEND systems, preparing the reader for purposeful monitoring and accountability. It empowers educators to think strategically and to define, refine and action their aspirations for leadership.

Key features include:

- An introduction to the 7 Ds of leadership – deliberate, dynamic, daring, dutiful, doable, developmental and distributive – which, when combined with the 7 Cs and Ps from the previous two books, places CPD at the heart of effective SEND leadership.
- An extensive SEND QA toolkit, leadership self-evaluation tools and an annual strategic planner.
- A SEND review audit framework with a Portfolio of Evidence and toolkit of materials including interview and observation schedules and questionnaires.
- An A–Z of adaptive teaching approaches.
- Case studies and testimonials from colleagues implementing the strengths-based language of the 7 Cs learning portfolio.

SEND Leadership can be read alongside *SEND Assessment* and *SEND Intervention*, or as a stand-alone resource, and supports SENCOs in their day-to-day roles. It will be a vital tool for SENCOs, teachers, TAs, governors and anyone else interested in providing effective SEN provision in educational settings.

Judith Carter is a registered Educational Psychologist (EP) and Director of Willow Tree Learning. She provides a range of bespoke training on SEND to individual schools, MATs and Local Authorities as well as hosting an Essential SENCO Network. Judith believes passionately in inclusion and education for all and works directly with staff, children, young people and their families, to promote participation and learning.

The Essential SENCO Toolkit Series

The Essential SENCO Toolkit is a series of books containing bespoke resources and frameworks for use by SENCOs and SEN practitioners. Each book contains a range of practical materials, tried-and-tested by members of the Essential SENCO Network. The author, Judith Carter, is an Educational Psychologist with over 20 years' experience. As the Director of Willow Tree Learning and host of the Essential SENCO Network she developed materials to respond directly to the needs expressed by practitioners. This original series provides a starting point to support the development of SEND Assessment, Intervention and Quality Assurance, offering clarity regarding the identification of SEN versus low attainment, and promoting resources to identify those learners with SEN, SEND, learners who are Disabled and those with Medical Needs. This series is essential reading and will aid practice development and offer support and encouragement to all who work in the profession.

Recent titles in the series include:

SEND Assessment
A Strengths-Based Framework for Learners with SEND
Judith Carter

SEND Intervention
Planning Provision with Purpose
Judith Carter

SEND Leadership
Quality Assuring Intent, Implementation and Impact
Judith Carter

For a complete list of titles in this series, please visit https://www.routledge.com/The-Essential-SENCO-Toolkit

SEND Leadership

Quality Assuring Intent, Implementation and Impact

JUDITH CARTER

Designed cover image: J Steer

First published 2025
by Routledge
4 Park Square, Milton Park, Abingdon, Oxon OX14 4RN

and by Routledge
605 Third Avenue, New York, NY 10158

Routledge is an imprint of the Taylor & Francis Group, an informa business

© 2025 Judith Carter

The right of Judith Carter to be identified as author of this work has been asserted in accordance with sections 77 and 78 of the Copyright, Designs and Patents Act 1988.

All rights reserved. The purchase of this copyright material confers the right on the purchasing institution to photocopy or download pages which bear the support material icon and a copyright line at the bottom of the page. No other parts of this book may be reprinted or reproduced or utilised in any form or by any electronic, mechanical, or other means, now known or hereafter invented, including photocopying and recording, or in any information storage or retrieval system, without permission in writing from the publishers.

Trademark notice: Product or corporate names may be trademarks or registered trademarks, and are used only for identification and explanation without intent to infringe.

British Library Cataloguing-in-Publication Data
A catalogue record for this book is available from the British Library

ISBN: 978-1-032-52886-1 (hbk)
ISBN: 978-1-032-52883-0 (pbk)
ISBN: 978-1-003-40899-4 (ebk)

DOI: 10.4324/9781003408994

Typeset in Bembo
by Deanta Global Publishing Services, Chennai, India

Access the Support Material: https://resourcecentre.routledge.com/speechmark

Contents

Acknowledgements viii

Introduction. 1

1 A shared language. 5

2 The 7 Ds of Leadership 18

3 Quality assurance 29

4 Intent 68

5 Implementation 90

6 Impact. 136

7 Practical management. 154

8 CPD 185

9 SEND LEADership 200

10 Getting started 212

References 231

Index. 233

Acknowledgements

This book is dedicated to all readers of *SEND Assessment* and *SEND Intervention* who have continued to enquire about Book 3! It has been great to know that some of you were 'waiting' for this book, and I thank you for your encouragement to write it. There have been times when I was not sure that the trilogy would ever be finished, but your hard work and creativity with the 7 Cs inspired me to carry on so thank you. I just hope the book is enjoyable to read and useful to you.

In particular, I would like to thank colleagues in Suffolk schools, settings and the Local Authority teams. It has been a pleasure to work directly with so many of you thanks to Suffolk County Council's commissioning of the Essential SENCO Toolkit for all schools and settings. It has been a joy to see the transformation of ideas into practice. Thanks to Claire Darwin, Maria Hough, Sonia Carrington, Ros Somerville, Carolyn Heyburn and Ivana Barron for their leadership and trust in this initiative. Ongoing thanks also to DNEAT academies and the wonderful leadership team, including Rachael Judd and Simon Morley. Also, to the Wensum Trust and Rachel Wilson, Academy Transformation Trust (ATT) and Abigail Joachim, St Benet's Trust and Nadine Avenal, Unity Trust, John Milton Academy Trust, Asset Trust, East Primary schools and of course to the many individual schools, settings and SENCOs, particularly Norfolk Colleagues and members of the Essential SENCO Network, who have shown such enthusiasm and creativity with these resources.

I would also like to thank my partner Matt Cooper and our yorkie-poodle dog Sunshine, aka Sunni, for their ongoing love and support and my Mum and Dad who have always encouraged me to do my best. Sadly, during the writing of this book, my Dad died, which as so many of you will know, is a life changing loss. As such, I would like to dedicate the book to the memory of my Dad, Tony Carter. It feels appropriate that my book about leadership is dedicated to him, as he was one of my first leadership role models. I didn't realise it at the time, but throughout my childhood I watched others follow my Dad's lead, without use of direction, discipline or force. Instead, he induced confidence, motivation and self-belief in others by showing compassion, humour and curiosity. Attributes truly worthy of a legacy.

Introduction

According to Microsoft 'Bing', the third film in a trilogy is called the threequel, so as this is technically the third book in the Essential SENCO Toolkit series, welcome to the threequel. Of course, if this is the first book from the series you are reading, you too are most welcome, and as each of the books has been written as a 'stand-alone' text, it is my intention that the information will be relevant and accessible to you regardless of prior reading. After all, you can watch *Star Wars: Return of the Jedi* without seeing the previous two films!

The advantage of reading the previous two books, however, is expectations. If you are familiar with my previous work, you will know that the intent of my writing is practical application. I am a huge fan of academic texts and indeed have learnt a great deal from many of them. However, these books are not those. Instead, this book, along with its predecessors, is practical in focus and is intended to offer you a 'starting point' for application. The wonderful thing about writing this book is that I am able to recall the incredible work that so many readers have undertaken with regard to the application of the 7 Cs Learning Portfolio and the 4 Functions of Learning Support. It has been such a privilege to work alongside many colleagues as they develop their own application of this approach and to hear of the implementation by others. Indeed, I am delighted to include some of their comments and experiences throughout the book, which I hope will further inspire you in your thinking and ongoing development. The contributors included in this book (listed in order of referencing) are:

- Alice North – SENCO, Bentley Primary School, Suffolk
- Vicki McClure – SENCO, Pulham Primary School
- Hannah Powley – EYFS/KS1 SENCO, St. Nicholas Priory CE VA Primary School
- Maria Adcock – Head of School and SENCO, Kingfisher Federation
- Sarah Smith – Deputy Head and SENCO, Kessingland Primary Academy
- Louise McGregor – SENDCO, Thurston CE Primary Academy
- Kathy Spurgeon – SENDCO, Federation of Fairfield Infant and Colneis Junior

- Emma Beck – SENDCO, Wells Primary and Nursery and Burnham Market Primary
- Jacqui Harris – SENDCO, Firside Junior School and Kinsale Junior School
- Allison McLellan – Vice Principal and SENCO, Hellesdon High School
- Donna Garratt – SENDCO, Acle St Edmund CE Primary Academy
- Jennie Gregson – SENCO, Arden Grove Infant and Nursery School
- Sally-Ann Hewitt-Coleman – SENCO, Open Academy
- Amy Healy – SENCO, Debenham High School
- Maryanne Peters – SENDCO and DSL, Diss Primary Academy and Scole CE Primary Academy
- Rachael Judd – Academies Group Executive Principal (AGEP), Diocese of Norwich Education and Academies Trust
- Abigail Joachim – SEND, Specialist Academy Transformation Trust
- Rachel Wilson – Educational Psychologist, Wensum Trust
- Nadine Avenal – SEND Lead, St. Benet's MAT

My thanks to these colleagues for sharing their work and experiences. It is the potential for our shared collaboration and ongoing development that motivates me to write, which I hope also motivates you to read. So, what can you expect from this book?

As the title suggests, our focus in this book is upon the leadership of SEND. At times the SENCO and/or SEN Practitioner role can become overwhelmingly operational in focus, with requests to return phone calls, respond to emails, meet with families, staff and external agencies, and to support learners who are in need. Everyday demands are huge and often unpredictable, and for so many SENCOs and SEN Practitioners, these responsibilities are just one of many professional 'hats' being worn. So, within this context, is it really possible to focus on strategy, leadership and quality assurance? The theme of this book is that yes, it is not only possible, but it is essential, as without a combined operational and strategic approach the demands of a SEND system will overwhelm even the most committed of professionals. *Leading* SEND systems is the only way to thrive as a SENCO or SEN Practitioner. **Operational management of SEND enables survival, but strategic leadership of SEND promotes a system that will thrive.** Over the next ten chapters, we will explore practical aspects of leadership and share resources that can support this process.

Introduction

Within our first chapter, I would like us to recap, or if this is the first book in the series you are reading, to explore, our shared language of SEN, SEND and medical needs, and to revise the purpose of the 7 Cs Learning Portfolio. I would also like us to revisit the 7 Ps of Provision so we can consider how SEND provision, previously defined as our 'action with intent', can be 'additional to or different from' adapted teaching. The rationale for this is that without a consistent and shared understanding of language, any collaborative actions have less potential. Without a consensus of understanding, leadership can become fragmented and disparate. In Chapter 2, I will introduce the 7 Ds of Leadership, written as an internal 'checklist' or prompt to aid your self-evaluation and ongoing reflections but also as a way of emphasising the importance of CPD as a tool for SENCOs and SEN Practitioners. When combined, the 7 Cs, 7 Ps and 7 Ds are intended to inspire your ongoing investment and protection of CPD both for yourself and for those around you. From here, we will explore quality assurance as a tool for SENCOs and SEN Practitioners and consider its origins and application. Chapter 3 also contains a quality assurance toolkit intended to provide an immediate starting point to aid you in your ongoing monitoring role. As always, please feel free to adapt or adopt these resources according to your needs and preferences.

The focus of Chapter 4 is the *intent* of the SEND system and where this can be seen. Chapter 5 will look at the *implementation* of the SEND system, including a bespoke approach to a self or peer review-audit of systems, via the collation of a portfolio of evidence. This will be followed by an exploration of the *impact* of the SEND system in Chapter 6. Chapter 7 is titled "Practical management" and, as the name suggests, will attempt to provide you with suggested starting points for ten potential actions for the leadership of the Essential SENCO Toolkit. In Chapter 8, we will revisit CPD and explore how this in itself is a tool for SEND leadership, which becomes our shared focus in Chapter 9. In Chapter 9, you will notice a change in letter formation regarding the word 'leadership', which will become LEADership. This will, I hope, act as a reminder that at the heart of SEND leadership is *Language*, *Empowerment*, *Ambition* and *Deliberateness*, which will be explored in detail. Finally, in Chapter 10, we will summarise and reflect and you can begin to identify your intended next steps, their implementation and your anticipated impact. Case study accounts will also be included here to further illustrate the potential for application. How does that sound? I hope it resonates with you and fulfils your expectations and interests. I also hope that despite not having any reference to Ewoks or unexpected familial relationships associated with the threequel film *Return of the Jedi*, it still motivates you to either continue reading one chapter at a time or helps you 'dip' into preferred chapters.

1. A shared language

The importance of establishing a shared language of SEND is a theme throughout the Essential SENCO Toolkit series of books and is featured here as a key attribute of SEND leadership. This is because without a consensus of understanding there cannot be clarity of direction, and without clarity of direction, there is no leadership. Even the definition of SEN and/or SEND can vary according to different practitioners and the 'to D or not to D' question with regards to SEN(D) is often a source of uncertainty. In Book 1, *SEND Assessment: A Strengths-based Framework for Learners with SEND*, time was spent acknowledging that SEND can in fact refer to three groups of learners. Those with a "learning difficulty that requires special educational provision", i.e. the Code of Practice 2015 definition of SEN; those who have a "physical and or mental impairment that has a long term, substantial adverse effect on day-to-day activities", i.e. the Equality Act 2010 definition of disability; and, of course, those learners who both have SEN and are disabled. The Venn diagram, originally published in "SEND Assessment", usefully presents this information, along with a further category of medical needs. It was the Children and Families Act 2014 that placed a duty on maintained schools and academies to "make arrangements to support pupils with medical conditions" (Code of Practice 2015, page 94). Learners with medical needs will include anyone who may require some form of medical action, such as the occasional use of an asthma inhaler, or someone who has a nut allergy. Accurate identification is essential as this should inform the action that is taken.

As leaders of SEND, SENCOs and SEN Practitioners need to ensure that staff are aware of the difference between a learner with SEND and a learner who is, for example, low attaining. Identifying a learner as having SEN is the equivalent of saying that they require provision that is "additional to or different from the curriculum made available to those of the same age". Therefore, for every learner identified as having SEN we should be able to account for the provision that is "additional to or different from". In comparison, a learner who is accessing the adapted curriculum but is lower attaining than some of their peers does not need "additional to or different from" and would not be identified as SEN. They would, of course, continue to be entitled to an adapted curriculum as part of the

DOI: 10.4324/9781003408994-2

provision that is 'ordinarily available' to others of the same age, which is, as the Teacher Standards remind us, the class and/or subject teachers' responsibility for all learners in their classes. But **an adapted curriculum is not the same as SEND provision.**

Within education we work incredibly hard to ensure that we can account for the intent, implementation and impact of our curriculum offer. We know that all learners are entitled to learning opportunities that are rich, relevant and diverse. We also know that we are tasked with ensuring access for all learners through the adaptation of materials and/or the modality of teaching that is offered. But if a teacher is offering an adapted curriculum for a learner with SEND, is that enough? Is that SEN provision? The argument presented here is that the adapted curriculum is the foundation on which SEN provision can be built, but it is not SEN provision itself. SEN provision is, after all, "additional to or different from" the curriculum offer. To help illustrate this, I encourage teachers to think of a picnic lunch box. Within the picnic box are sandwiches, fruit, yoghurt, crisps and a drink. In many ways, our curriculum offer is the 'bread and butter' of teaching and represents the basis of our sandwich. As mentioned above, we work hard to ensure that we use the very best 'quality' bread for our sandwiches or our curriculum offer, and it is adapted or personalised relevant to learner starting points in the same way as a sandwich will differ in its fillings according to tastes. Some sandwiches will use granary bread, wholemeal, white or sourdough bread (a choice that would have emerged from your staff conversations about the quality and intent of your curriculum). And this bread will be used to create sandwiches that may contain cheese and tomato, ham and coleslaw or prawn mayonnaise, and so the options go on. In this analogy the sandwich filling represents the adaptions that the teacher makes to the curriculum offer to ensure the inclusion of all learners in their class(es). However, the SEN provision is 'additional to or different from' this, so can be viewed as the yoghurt in our picnic lunch box example. The sandwiches have been adapted according to learner taste (needs) as this is their curriculum entitlement, but if a learner has SEN then they are also entitled to a yoghurt! The yoghurt is not instead of the sandwich; it is in addition to it. Continuing this analogy, the fruit can represent additional and targeted provision linked to pupil premium, and the crisps could be 'COVID-19 catch up' funding or indeed any other additional provisions that you offer.

The purpose of the picnic lunch box analogy is to clarify the distinction between adaptive teaching and SEN provision. In the second book of the Essential SENCO

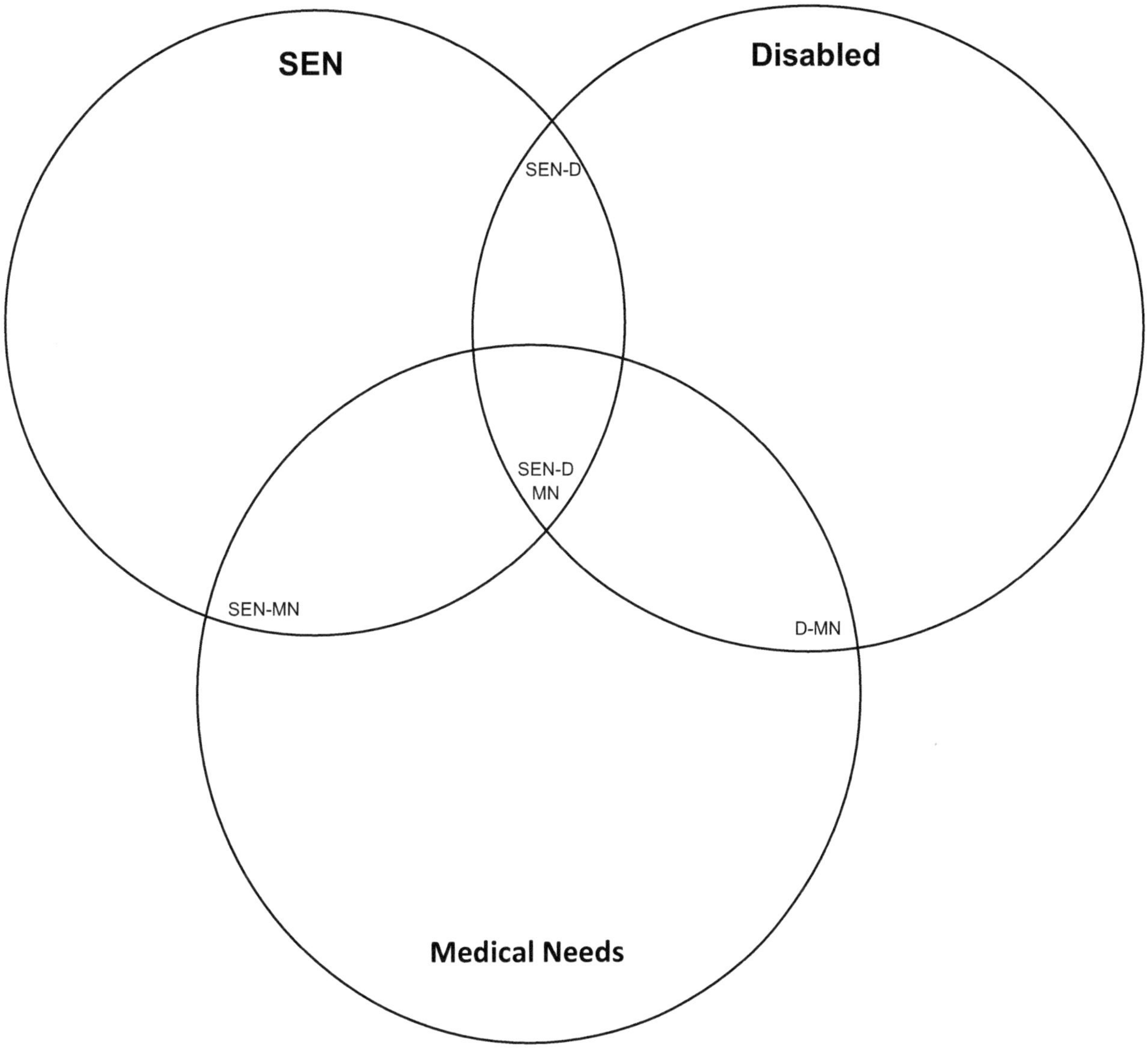
SEN
Disabled
SEN-D
SEN-D
MN
SEN-MN
D-MN
Medical Needs

Key Definitions:

"A child has a special educational need if they have a learning difficulty that requires special educational provision". (Code of Practice 2014)

A person is disabled if they have "a physical or mental impairment which has a long-term and substantial adverse effect on their ability to carry out normal day-to-day activities". (Equality Act 2010)

Toolkit series, *SEND Intervention: Planning Provision with Purpose*, I define provision as "action with intent". Intent either to overcome a barrier to learning or, if possible, to remove a barrier to learning. For example, if a learner has reading as a barrier to learning, during a science lesson we would try to overcome that barrier to enable access to the science lesson. This might include ensuring that the learner has verbal instructions instead of written text, or we may ask an adult or another learner to read the written instructions to the learner. If we have reading/scanning pens or read-aloud text, we may use these. All of the above are effective strategies for overcoming the barrier to learning. But at some point, we want to teach the learner to read, because if we teach them to read, we remove the barrier. It is important to recognise that not all barriers can or indeed should be removed. For example, there is nothing 'wrong' with an autistic learner; they simply experience a different way of being, so we should not or indeed could not try to 'remove' autism, but we would try to overcome any barriers limiting participation. Whilst reflecting on the importance of language, let us also take a moment to consider how we describe learners. Would you describe a learner on your SEND record as 'a learner with SEND' or a 'SEND learner'? Do you opt for the person-first model, hence a 'person with an impairment' or an 'impaired person'? My practice has always been to opt for the person-first model. I regularly feel uncomfortable with the phrase 'SEND child' as, for me personally, I believe children are children are children! A SEND child sounds like a different variant of a human being, which I do not believe in. That said, you may have noticed that I referred to an 'autistic learner' rather than using the term 'learner with autism'. The reason for this is that the reported preference of the autistic community, rather like the deaf community, is that this is their preferred term. As such, I would always want to respect and comply with this, which is why it is essential that within our roles we seek clarity of language from individual children, young people and adults. As ultimately, in the same way as we are now respecting individual preferences for pronoun use, so we should remain mindful of our language when describing individuals and groups.

Overcoming or, if possible, removing barriers to learning is our action with intent or our SEN provision. It is a balance of adjustments, support/resources and or interventions. It is this that is our yoghurt, or our 'additional to or different from'. The adapted curriculum, or sandwich, continues to be personalised for the learner, but the SEN provision should not be 'more of the same'. If a learner is falling behind in maths, we work with the learner, their family and staff to identify why we think they are falling behind in maths. We don't just give them more maths. And we don't just give them more maths because they are *already* receiving more maths — that is their adapted curriculum offer (or sandwich). If we think they are falling behind in maths because of a special educational need, we attempt to identify the barriers to learning and then offer provision to overcome and/or remove these. The 7 Cs Learning Portfolio provides a language for SEND identification which in turn helps to define the provision that can be offered. Within Book 1, *SEND Assessment: A Strengths-Based Framework for Learners with SEND*, the 7 Cs Learning Portfolio introduced seven concepts beginning with the letter C. Curriculum was placed in the centre, but skills relating to cognition, communication, creativity, control, compassion and co-ordination were also included. Within each of the seven concepts are a further seven learning attributes, meaning that the 7 Cs Learning Portfolio provides teachers, teaching assistants, learners and their families with a language of 49 attributes that can be considered strengths or areas for development. Indeed, it is the identification of three strengths and three areas for development that many readers have used as their starting point in the implementation of this framework.

> The essential toolkit is a valuable tool. It really focuses on the child's strengths which can be overlooked when a child presents with SEND. It is an effective structure which has created a robust system in our schools to support early identification. It has equipped staff with a shared understanding and language. It provides a structured framework for staff to profile children; it has supported our understanding of their individual barriers and provides strategies to overcome and remove these barriers.
>
> *(Alice North – SENCO at Bentley School, Suffolk)*

The 7 Cs Learning Portfolio sheet provides the A4 booklet containing all of the 49 learning attributes. It is presented in this format so a copy of the grid can be printed or photocopied and then folded to create a useful booklet of the 7 Cs. If you have the electronic materials, print off a paper copy of this sheet and hold it in a landscape position. Fold the paper in half and then fold it again and again. At this point focus on the quality of your folds, ensuring that the corners are as accurate as possible, and then open the sheet to its original size. From here, hold the paper in a portrait position and fold the paper down, so the fold is along the top. Cut along the line, down the fold, so you create a slit in the paper for one section and then open the sheet again. This time hold the sheet in a landscape position and fold it in the middle, pushing the sides together. (The slit should make a square.) Keep pushing the paper together and fold the pages around to make the book. You

7 Cs Learning Portfolio

Cognition
- Working Memory
- Speed of Processing
- Inference
- Anticipation
- Reflection
- Evaluation
- Analysis

Communication
- Speech - Expressive Vocab
  - Articulation
- Language - Understanding Vocab
- Collaborative Conversation
- Listening - Follow Instructions
- Social Communication (Output)
- Social Interaction (Input)

Curriculum
- English
  - ➤ Reading
  - ➤ Writing
  - ➤ Spelling
- Math
  - ➤ Number
  - ➤ Shape/Space
- Science
- Art & Music
- History & Geography
- Computing
- PE & Sport

Co-ordination
- Fine Motor - Handwriting, Cutting, Threading
- Gross Motor - Jumping, Hopping, Kick, Catch, Throw a Ball
- Sensory – vision, hearing, tracking
- Mobility
- Stability + Balance
- Posture
- Sensory Processing

Creativity
- Generate Ideas
- Problem Solving
- Attention
- Motivation
- Making Things
- Courage-Determination
- Trust

Compassion
- Friendships
- Turn Taking
- Empathy
- Sense of Justice
- Self Esteem & Wellbeing
- Self Efficacy
- Support for Others

Control
- Self Regulation
- Behaviour for Learning
- Anxiety Management
- Confidence
- Resilience
- Language of Emotions
- Independence

Copyright material from Judith Carter (2025), *SEND Leadership*, Routledge

should now have a pocket-sized prompt of the 7 Cs Learning Portfolio. I have made these books with staff in many staff meetings, both face-to-face and during online training days, and this practical prompt is often cited as a preferred resource from the toolkit, which I hope is your experience too.

If you like the 7 Cs Learning Portfolio A4 sheet, I am confident that you will also like the Adapted Teaching A–Z prompt booklet. If not, I can only apologise! This booklet is made in the same way but helps teachers to identify adaptive teaching approaches to use with all learners (not just those with SEND). It is most effective when introduced as part of staff training on adaptive teaching and SEND provision. I have found that a visual picnic lunchbox is a powerful aid in explaining the difference between the bread and butter of the curriculum offer and the personalised sandwich that they create as part of their adapted teaching. This then sets up the introduction of the yoghurt as the "additional to or different from" SEN provision. The A–Z can be used to promote conversations about adaptions that are made for all learners, and the 7 Cs Learning Portfolio can provide a language of SEND assessment and SEND provision. To aid the A–Z conversations, I have also included a summary sheet.

As with all work presented in the Essential SENCO Toolkit, it is offered as a starting point and is not attempting to be a definitive solution. The A–Z is intended to promote discussion and reflection and to encourage staff to define the tweaks and adaptions that they make for all learners.

A – Adjust – This refers to the tweaks an adult may make in response to the learner's reaction or needs. We can adjust the methods we use to present information, for example, choosing to provide verbal instructions instead of written instructions to a learner who finds reading difficult.

B – Baseline – Adaptive teaching requires knowledge of starting points so that the adult can plan ambitious and accessible learning experiences relative to these starting points.

C – Collaboration – Adults will promote opportunities for collaborative work between peers and with themselves.

D – Direct Instruction – This is when we make explicit the implicit, and we provide clarity and structure to information.

E – Exemplar – Adults will use examples or models to promote understanding and offer clarity of expectations.

F – Flexible Groupings – The opportunity to mix learners and promote movement and challenge alongside different peers.

G – Games – The use of games can aid motivation and provide wonderful opportunities for rehearsal and reinforcement of skills.

H – Highlight – Both in terms of highlighting and emphasising information or key points, but also using visual highlights to aid identification and application.

I – Indicate – This refers to the importance of advanced warnings and reminders which aid focus and remind learners of the time remaining.

J – Justify – Where we provide a rationale and purpose for the task, explicitly defining its intent, or describing connections and applications of the transcendence of information.

K – Key Vocabulary – Ensuring access to key words visually whilst also verbally reminding and revising the meaning of words.

L – Listen – At the heart of adaptive teaching is listening, whether that is listening to words or actions, or the expression of feelings as communication. It is an essential tool for assessment.

M – Mind Maps – These can provide visual scaffolds and structures to aid sequencing and prompt recall.

N – Now and Next – Verbalising or visually representing immediate actions and expectations alongside next steps to aid the sense of context.

O – Options – Adults can ensure that learners have different methods for recording or demonstrating their learning, either through writing, typing, filming, voice recording or collaboration with another.

P – Paraphrase – Checking out the learner's understanding of a task or information by asking them to rephrase or summarise their perception.

Q – Question – This refers to the practice of using questions rather than giving answers, which in itself promotes thinking, ownership and connections.

R – Recap – Where adults encourage the revision of prior learning and clarify its relevance and application.

S – Scaffold – The provision of prompts or support which enables access to the next stage of learning.

T – Technology – How we encourage the use and deployment of technology to promote independent recording, research and learning.

U – Update – Adults can interleave learning and remind learners of the purpose or intent of a task or learning experience and the time remaining.

V – Visuals – Combining visual images or examples alongside spoken instructions to promote greater understanding and connections.

W – Word Banks – Adults can provide personalised word banks for individual learners or create subject word lists that can be used as a reference point, aiding the development of independent learning.

X – eXcite – It is essential that adults teach with enthusiasm and relevance and promote the sharing of knowledge as a joy and a privilege.

Y – Yield – Although at first glance this may appear somewhat controversial, it is a reminder that adaptive teaching is about flexibility and responsiveness. As the adults we are equipped for such change and we should adapt to the needs of learners rather than retaining a rigidity of approach.

Z – Zone – This refers to the creation of learning areas or spaces within the environment that can be adapted to maximise learning opportunities and enable personalisation and adaption.

A-Z of Adaptive Teaching Practical Prompts

Willow Tree Learning

A – Adjust
B – Baseline
C – Collaboration
D – Direct Instruction

E – Exemplar
F – Flexible groupings
G – Games
H – Highlight

I – Indicate
J – Justify
K – Key Vocabulary
L – Listen

M – Mind maps
N – Now & Next
O – Options
P – Paraphrase

Q – Question
R – Recap
S – Scaffold
T – Technology

U – Update
V – Visuals
W – Word banks

X – eXcite
Y – Yield
Z – Zone

Copyright material from Judith Carter (2025), *SEND Leadership*, Routledge

A–Z of adaptive teaching

Practice prompts

A – Adjust – Respond to a learner's reaction and tweak information as necessary.

B – Baseline – Know the starting point for each learner and plan ambitious learning relative to the starting point.

C – Collaboration – Promote collaborative work between peers and/or adults.

D – Direct Instruction – Clarity of information and explicit teaching.

E – Exemplar – Provide examples or models to promote understanding of expectations.

F – Flexible Groupings – Mix learners and promote movement and challenge.

G – Games – Use games to promote rehearsal and reinforcement.

H – Highlight – Verbally emphasise information and visually highlight important points.

I – Indicate – Give warnings and remind learners of the time remaining and expectations.

J – Justify – Provide a rationale and purpose for the task and explicitly describe connections and applications.

K – Key Vocabulary – Ensure access to key words visually and revisit meaning.

L – Listen – Listen to words, actions and feelings expressed by learners as part of ongoing assessment.

M – Mind Maps – Provide visual scaffolds and maps to aid sequencing and prompt recall.

N – Now and Next – Explicitly label immediate steps and what happens next.

O – Options – Ensure that learners have options for presentation and engagement, relative to the starting points.

P – Paraphrase – Check out the learners' understanding by asking them to summarise what they are doing and why.

Q – Question – Use questions rather than give answers, promote thinking and application.

R – Recap – Revise prior learning and clarify its relevance.

S – Scaffold – Prompt and support access to the next stage of learning.

T – Technology – Use technology to promote independent recording and research.

U – Update – Interleave learning and remind learners of the purpose and time remaining.

V – Visuals – Use visuals alongside spoken instructions and during task completion.

W – Word banks – Promote the development of personalised word banks and reference points for independent learning.

X – eXcite – Teach with enthusiasm and relevance, promoting the sharing of knowledge as a joy and privilege.

Y – Yield – Remain flexible and adapt to the needs of the learner rather than retaining rigid expectations.

Z – Zone – Promote learning areas or spaces within the environment and create recording zones to support presentations.

The inclusion of these resources is intended to support you in establishing a shared language of SEND and to clarify the building blocks of an adaptive or inclusive curriculum as the foundation of any personalised SEND provision. Such clarity is an essential attribute for effective SEND leadership. Unless there is a consensus of understanding shared by all members of your school or academy community, your attempts to lead SEND in your setting will be fraught with confusion and uncertainty. Make explicit the implicit and go back to basics, ensuring that everyone has a shared language and clarity of expectations.

Reflections

- Is there a shared language of SEN, SEND and medical needs within your setting? Do all staff 'know' how and why to identify a learner as having SEN(D)?
- Is there clarity of understanding about the difference between an inclusive adapted curriculum and SEN provision?
- Do staff, learners and their families have a shared language of learning, such as that provided by the 7 Cs Learning Portfolio?
- Can they use this shared language to identify strengths and areas for development?
- Is there a shared understanding of SEN support and do all learners identified as requiring SEN support receive provision that is additional to or different from?

Actions to consider

- Introduce the SEN, SEND, MN Venn diagram to staff and promote a conversation about the how and why of accurate identification.
- Use the A–Z of adaptive teaching to scaffold the sharing of practice regarding adaptive teaching. Reinforce that adaptive teaching is the personalised sandwich making and SEND provision is the yoghurt, i.e. additional to or different from the adaptive curriculum offer that is ordinarily available to all learners.
- Listen out for the language used to describe learners and notice language in written policies and your SEN Information Report. Look for inconsistencies and reflect on preferred terminology.

2. The 7 Ds of Leadership

Those of you familiar with *SEND Assessment: A Strengths-based Framework for Learners with SEND* and *SEND Intervention: Planning Provision with Purpose* will recall the 7 Cs Learning Portfolio and the 7 Ps of Provision, and will, I hope, smile at the introduction of the 7 Ds of Leadership (Figure 2.1). Not only am I attempting to connect the three books via the 7 Cs, Ps and Ds concepts, but I am also promoting key principles for SEND leadership within the 7 Ds Framework. In addition, I am attempting to emphasise the importance of 'CPD' as a tool for leaders by bringing each of these together.

The purpose of the 7 Ds is to provide you with a reference point for evaluating your own leadership approaches in SEND and those of the other leaders around you. The intention is to encourage you to mindfully 'lead' within your role and to really consider what this means to you. Over the years, I have worked with many leaders who have inspired me either to want to emulate their approach or indeed to eliminate their approach from any aspect of mine or anyone else's lived experience! It is true, leadership is inspirational one way or another. I think it is safe to assume that we share the ambition of being leaders that others will want to emulate rather than eliminate! And, of course, SEND leadership is about the leadership of a system that includes provision that will ultimately impact the life outcomes of learners and their families, not to mention the other adults and learners operating within the system too. The phrase 'no pressure' feels particularly inappropriate for this description because, in fact, leading a SEND system is full of pressure in every sense of the phrase. Pressure to get it right, pressure on those working within it, pressure externally and internally, not to mention the pressure you may feel at times as an individual SENCO or SEN Practitioner. Is it really a coincidence that the word 'lead' is spelt the same way as the word 'lead', as in a 'lead weight?' At times, the SENCO role can feel like a lead weight with its relentless demands and ever-changing context. So how can you assimilate that pressure and convert it into energy for leadership?

DOI: 10.4324/9781003408994-3

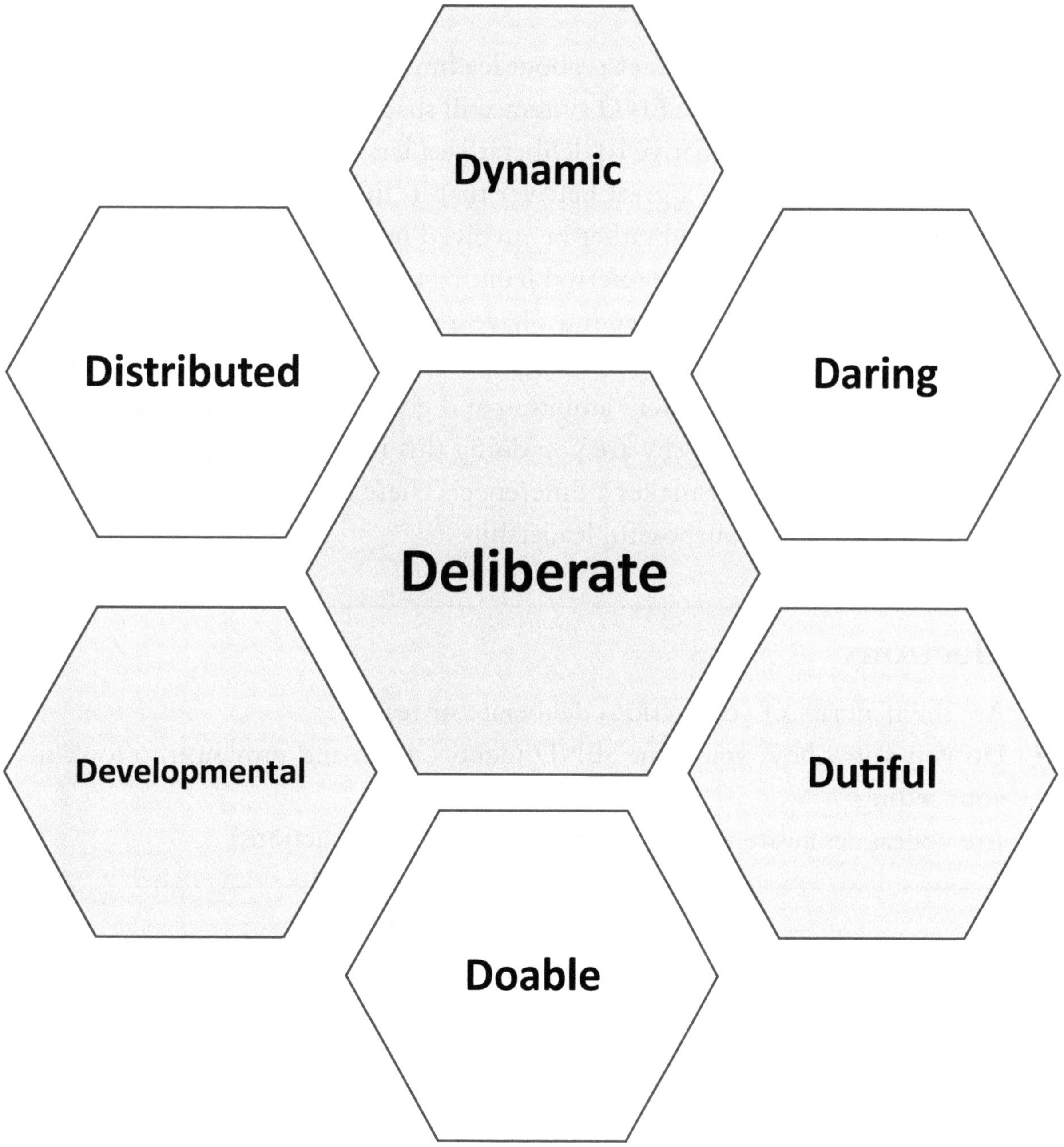

- Dynamic
- Distributed
- Daring
- **Deliberate**
- Developmental
- Dutiful
- Doable

Converting any source of stress into energy requires clarity of purpose. The importance of clarity is referred to within the first of our 7 Ds of Leadership: Deliberate.

Deliberate leadership

Deliberate leadership in this context is about leading with intent. Having a clear vision and an ambition for the SEND system will shape your actions and those of others around you. The alternative to deliberate leadership is reactive or accidental leadership, and although I am a great believer that if 'life gives you lemons, you should make lemonade', I would rather be involved in the conversation about whether lemons are, in fact, our preferred fruit for the season. In real terms, as SENCOs and SEN Practitioners, we must have a plan for SEND identification, provision and development. If not us, then whom? Deliberate leadership involves reflection, consideration, aspiration, ambition and good-old solution-focused 'hope'. What are you doing? Why are you doing this instead of something else? And how will you know if it makes a difference? These are the questions that can help to form deliberate or purposeful leadership.

> **Reflections**
> - Are the majority of your actions deliberate or reactive?
> - Do you know how you want SEND identification and provision to look in your setting?
> - Are colleagues aware of the deliberate nature of your actions?

Dynamic leadership

The second of our 7 Ds is dynamic leadership. The Cambridge Dictionary defines dynamic as "having lots of ideas and enthusiasm" and "continuously changing or developing". It also describes dynamic as being "full of energy", so as Meatloaf famously sung, "two out of three ain't bad!" Seriously though, even if we don't always feel full of energy due to the relentless demands of our work, our approach to leadership can remain energised and positive. To me, dynamic leadership ultimately encourages us to lead with enthusiasm and interaction. It is easier to adopt an enthusiastic approach when there is shared clarity of purpose and aspiration. Without it, one person's enthusiasm can become another person's source of frustration, which in turn can lead to disconnect and disparity. When I think of dynamic leaders that I have worked with, I felt reassured by the clarity of their vision and inspired by their optimism and pace. I believed in them and felt like a valued contributor to the journey, so began to believe in 'us'. In comparison, leaders without a dynamic and interactive style tended to isolate and become isolated, creating a culture of uncertainty and disappointment.

> **Reflections**
> - Do you enjoy your work?
> - Are you surrounded by enthusiastic or resentful leaders?
> - Does your setting 'feel' dynamic at its heart?

Daring leadership

In my experience the most effective leaders are those with courage and determination. Again, I believe that courage is rooted in clarity of purpose and vision and underpinned by values. The Code of Practice 2015 uses the phrase "best endeavours" when describing the expected actions of all settings when meeting the needs of learners with SEND. This is as relevant a phrase for SEND leadership as it is for provision. It is essential that as leaders we give our best endeavours, which will often require courage and daring. Leading SEND, especially within a self-declared 'broken, but trying to heal itself' national system, is quite the challenge! We may not be jumping out of aeroplanes or climbing physical mountains on a daily basis, but our work is no less of a challenge. Forget 'boldly going where no-one has gone before', try to keep going down the same frustrating 'rabbit hole' day in and day out; that is true courage! So much of the SEND system is frustrating and irritating and unbelievably time-consuming, yet SEND leaders continue to champion and dare to work towards a better system for learners and their families. Striving to shape and refine the SEND system is daring leadership.

> **Reflections**
> - What are your aspirations for SEND in your setting?
> - Who have you shared your aspirations with?
> - If there was a magic wand, what would you dare to wish for learners with SEND in your setting?

Dutiful leadership

The fourth of our 7 Ds is dutiful leadership. This acknowledges the importance of compliance with national and legal frameworks. There is a vast array of 'musts' within any Code of Practice, and the 2015 Code is no exception. Understanding the SEND system is essential, both to deliver entitlements to learners and their families and to do the job. There are huge issues around accountability within our work, which in themselves can determine the direction of our leadership. But in addition to our compliance with existing requirements, as professionals working within the system, we also have an opportunity or, dare I say, a duty to champion change and facilitate future developments. Our SEND systems do not operate in a vacuum but are part of a wider education system, and our voices need to shape that system. Where you can, actively seek to participate, shape and contribute to the development of our national and local SEND systems. After all, you have an insight and reality that needs to shape national and local policy. You have the potential to advocate, champion and support learners and their families, and to call out systemic strengths and areas for development. Of course, fulfil your duties with regards to compliance but remember, change can be most effective from within. Keep asking questions, sharing experiences and promoting systemic reflection as to why it is this way.

> **Reflections**
> - Is your voice heard?
> - Would you like it to be louder?
> - What do you want to say?

Doable leadership

Doable leadership acknowledges the importance of pragmatism and relevance. As a leader your workload, and the workload of those around you, must be doable or else you will burn out. The reality for many SENCOs and SEN Practitioners, is that the demands of the job do not match the time that has been allocated. This can become a major source of stress and anxiety and can utterly debilitate brilliant professionals through no fault of their own. If you feel that there is no time for leadership, or indeed, feel that there is no time, it is essential that you discuss this with your line manager, SEN governor and or the leadership team. A useful approach is to account for what *can* be done in the time available, and what else *could* be done with additional time. This removes the burden of perceived failure from an individual and gives it back to the system. Collectively, system leaders then at least have knowledge and can consider options. It is not always possible to fund additional time, but at least system leaders are aware of gaps and can look to action improvements in time. For you, as a leader of SEND, your focus needs to be on pursuing development whilst ensuring initiatives are perceived to be achievable or doable by those you are leading. Your deliberate leadership must contain a vision that is aspirational *and* achievable, or else those you are attempting to lead will lose faith and trust, and you may ultimately lose 'you' in the process. Those SMART targets of the past (specific, measurable, achievable, relevant and time-related) are highly relevant to our practice as leaders of SEND. An essential part of SEND leadership is self-motivation and self-care alongside support and well-being for our colleagues, learners and their families. Without these, there may not be anyone to lead or anyone waiting to be led.

> **Reflections**
> - How many weekends do you end up working in a month?
> - Are you encouraged to maintain a work–life balance and to take care of yourself?
> - Is this also true for other leaders and staff in your setting?

Developmental leadership

Developmental leadership is the sixth of our 7 Ds, and it is included to remind all leaders that the ultimate purpose of leadership is to build capacity beyond oneself. Leadership should build capacity and maximise the strengths of all contributors to the system valuing each and every participant. With regards to the SEND system, we should be developing approaches that extend and improve our knowledge, understanding and practice. We should build capacity in those around us who, in turn, will develop and extend us in a positive cycle of growth. Take a moment to reflect on a recent initiative that you have introduced to your setting or has been introduced. Has it added value and empowered others? Why was it introduced? Was there a shared need for this, so it was commissioned on behalf of everyone, or were colleagues told that they needed this? Has this initiative changed your practice or thinking? Will you and others remember this in a month, six months or a year? What were the developmental outcomes from this?

As a leader promoting development, it is essential that you remain focused on what it is that you are trying to develop. Why are you are trying to develop this instead of something else, and how will you know it makes a difference? What will it look like? What purpose will it serve? How will it affect change for learners, families, staff or the system as a whole? Shared developmental outcomes have the potential to empower and build capacity, which can be a useful goal of leadership, but only if there is clarity regarding purpose and anticipated impact.

> **Reflections**
> - Where can you see changes?
> - Who has grown and developed as a result of your leadership of SEND?
> - Who do you want to grow and develop as a result of your leadership?

Distributed leadership

Our final D is distributed leadership. At the heart of this principle is collaboration and sharing. An effective leader cannot, or should not, 'do' everything themselves. Instead, deliberate delegation, collaboration and a sharing of ideas and opportunities for development are required. Enabling the participation of all is central to effective leadership, and no more so than when leading a SEND system. Promoting shared ownership for the development of an inclusive culture of teaching and learning will do more for your SEND system than any form, referral or target! Supporting staff to maximise their participation and contribution to the graduated approach will not only help them to meet their responsibilities but also empower them to understand why this is a requirement. However skilled you are as a SENCO or SEN Practitioner, you cannot and should not fulfil or replace the roles of other colleagues in the SEND process. Distribute your leadership skills through the engagement of others.

In real terms this can be achieved through conversations, shared activities, training and the distribution of daily tasks. Talking and, essentially, listening are tools for leadership, but it is a balance between talking and listening, with more time spent listening, that will bring about change.

> **Reflections**
> - How confident are staff to complete SEN support cycles and/or annual reviews?
> - How engaged are staff, governors, leaders, families and learners with the co-production of the SEN Information Report and, where appropriate, the SEN policy?
> - How active are leaders and governors in the quality assurance of SEND identification and provision?

The purpose of the 7 Ds of Leadership is to encourage your own thinking around the characteristics of effective leadership and to offer you a starting point as you navigate the tools and approaches in this book. The Leadership Self-Evaluation form contains some further questions to encourage reflection and evaluation about where you are as a leader of SEND and, importantly, where you want to be. When time allows, consider these questions and how they resonate with you. It is not a test and there are no right or wrong responses, just information that will hopefully help you to connect with your leadership baseline. For those of you who are more visual in your reflections, I would encourage you to consider replicating a 'Pinterest'-type board of the positive attributes of an inspiring leader, and the negative attributes. Creating a visual board or word wall can help to define our core constructs regarding leadership and help to shape what we want to emulate and/or eliminate from our own practice.

Leadership Self-Evaluation

The purpose of these questions is to encourage reflection on your strengths and the areas you want to develop as a leader.

1. Write down five key attributes that you think good leaders have.

2. Use a rating scale of numbers 1–10, where 10 is the highest and 1 is the lowest, to allocate a number indicating where you think you are with regards to each of these attributes.

3. Put these attributes in rank order of importance to you.

4. Why have you created this order?

5. Identify three strengths and three areas for development about you as a leader.

   Strengths

   Areas for development

6. Do you think colleagues would identify the same things? Can you ask any of them?

7. Why do you want to be an effective leader?

8. What is the change that you would like to bring about?

9. Use a rating scale of numbers 1–10, where 10 is the highest and 1 is the lowest, and allocate your own score against each of the 7 Ds of leadership.

Deliberate	Doable
Dynamic	Developmental
Daring	Distributed
Dutiful	

10. Do you want to change any of these? If yes, what steps could you take?

As we shift our focus onto quality assurance, evaluation of intent, implementation and impact of SEND systems in the next few chapters, remember the 7 Ds, and consider how you could use these suggestions deliberately, dynamically, with daring whilst complying to duties and still ensure that your leadership remains doable, developmental and distributed. If you can do that whilst keeping your head when those around you are losing theirs, yours is the world (of SEND) and everything in it, and you will be a SENCO/SEN Practitioner my friend!

> **Actions to consider**
> - Discuss leadership attributes within a senior leadership meeting and/or staff meeting and share the 7 Ds of leadership hexagon. Identify strengths and areas for development.
> - Use the reflective questions in the 'about me as a leader' sheet to identify three strengths and three areas for development.
> - Look for evidence of each of the 7 Ds within your leadership approach to SEND during an academic year. Note them down.

3. Quality assurance

Quality assurance (QA) as a process is an essential leadership tool. It involves 'testing' or 'checking out' systems and exploring whether the actual impact shares any similarity with the anticipated impact. For SENCOs and SEN Practitioners, quality assurance refers to any actions that are taken to explore the effectiveness of the SEND system. **As leaders, you define the intent of the SEND system, promote its implementation and evaluate its impact. As part of this evaluation, you consider the consistency accuracy and effectiveness of the systems.** As such, in real terms, **quality assurance refers to the methods we apply to evaluate whether what we 'think' is happening, is actually happening, and if it is, whether the actual impact is as we anticipated.** Twinkl (2023, available at https://www.twinkl.co.uk/teaching-wiki/quality-assurance) state that:

> Quality assurance is used to carry out quality management and is a method to help make sure certain quality standards are fulfilled.

They go on to say that:

> Quality assurance is important for schools to help them maintain and improve their efficiency, leadership and students' progress by self and external assessments. By working towards quality assurance standards, schools will be ensuring that both staff and students support high-quality inclusive teaching and learning.

Such tools are an essential part of SEND leadership. The Code of Practice 2015 states that:

> Schools support pupils with a wide range of SEN. They should regularly review and evaluate the breadth and impact of the support they offer or can access.

(page 93)

DOI: 10.4324/9781003408994-4

The importance of evaluating the effectiveness of provision made for learners is also stated as a required descriptor of the SEN Information Report within the Code of Practice 2015, where it provides 14 bullet points that must be included in the SEN Information Report (page 106–107). Yet, so often, time for quality assurance activities evades the weekly priorities of SENCOs and SEN Practitioners. This is not because of a lack of commitment or understanding of the importance of the tasks, but simply a result of excessive time pressures and operational priorities. For so many SENCOs and SEN Practitioners there is quite simply not enough time for the 'day job', meaning the operational implementation of the SEN policy and other duties that may have been combined with the role. As a result, the strategic quality assurance tasks, or 'litmus testing' of the SEND system may become a regular 'carry forward' of the weekly or monthly 'to-do' list. Sadly, this chapter does not contain a 'secret spell' for creating more time or a formula for the 'cloning' of ourselves or indeed time travel. So, what is offered? The focus will be upon five themes that may help to locate a starting point for the adoption of regular monitoring and quality assurance tasks, including the provision of a SENCO QA Toolkit. The suggestions included here are offered with genuine empathy for the demands on time associated with the SENCO and SEN Practitioner role. The intention is that some of these suggestions may help you to adopt a 'little but often' approach to quality assurance and limit the panic that can be associated with waking up in the early hours remembering that such and such has not been done.

1. QA methodology

Methodology is one of those words that we associate with research and often with writing assignments. Yet, in fact, its relevance to our SEND leadership role is immense. Utilising our prior knowledge of research methods can help us define short but regular tasks that will help us to evaluate the effectiveness of our SEND systems. For example, observation. A learning walk or a learning support walk can help us to notice strengths or areas for development regarding the implementation of our expectations for SEND provision. Protecting time to complete themed learning support walks can help SENCOs and SEN Practitioners evaluate the quality of adult questioning when working with learners or review the accessibility of visual aids to support learning. The identification of specific themes for observation will depend on your current priorities and recent CPD opportunities. But it could include the following:

- The contribution of additional adults on learning via the implementation of the 4 Functions of Learning Support: During the learning support walk, were TAs providing mediation, reinforcement of a skill or a learning behaviour, carrying out an assessment or facilitating an intervention?
- Learner ownership of support plans or help-me prompts: During the observed learning support walk, were any learner passports, targeted outcome bookmarks, or help-me cards visible or actively being used by learners?
- Use of adjustment and or support/resources menus: During the learning support walk, highlight adjustments observed from the adjustment menu sheet.

Interviewing is another research method that can be used as part of your quality assurance information gathering toolkit. These can be structured or semi-structured interviews that are voice-recorded or scribed and could include:

- Interviewing individuals or a small group of learners with SEND to review their experiences of types of SEND provision, including adjustments, use of support and resources and what they have gained from interventions.
- Telephone interviews with individual family members of learners with SEND and or a small focus group of parents and/or carers to elicit views about the quality and impact of SEND provision.
- Focus group with teachers and/or TAs gathering views on the implementation of and impact of SEND provision.

Electronic or paper-based questionnaires can also be utilised as a means of gathering information from essential 'users' of the SEND system to aid our understanding of the effectiveness of approaches. Including:

- Questions for families of learners with SEND eliciting confidence and perceptions regarding the quality and diversity of SEN Support provided by the setting.
- Verbal or visual questions for learners receiving SEN Support exploring their views of the relevance and usefulness of provision.
- Teacher and or TA questionnaire auditing perceived skills and confidence regarding a specific aspect of SEN provision.

Once again, there are no right or wrong methods for quality assurance, but rather only your preferred methods. The key is to triangulate information, eliciting information from learners, their families, teachers, TAs and, of course, your own information gathered through the inevitable participant observation associated with your role. The SEND Quality Assurance Toolkit contains information gathering schedules that can be used and or adapted as part of your work. There is no expectation that you alone would be completing these tasks and certainly not all at once or in one half term. Think about the 7 Ds of leadership and remember, distributed leadership specifically. It may be that you can ask other members of the senior leadership team to undertake some activities during the year either alone or alongside you. Also keep in mind that according to the 7 Ds of Leadership, our actions need to be 'doable' so consider developing a plan where short but regular amounts of time can be allocated for QA and monitoring. Familiarise yourself with the QA toolkit so you can begin to consider how and when these tasks can be undertaken during a year.

SEND Quality Assurance Toolkit

Contents

QA Method	Tool	Application
Observation	Learning Support Walk	Complete during themed learning walks
Observation	SEN Information Report Practical Application	Identify a theme and look for evidence in a learning walk
Observation	Learner engagement	Observation schedule for use with sample learners
Interview	Learner evaluation	Focus group or individual learner discussion
	Family consultation	Focus group or phone consultation with families
	Teacher evaluation	Focus group or individual teacher discussion
	TA evaluation	Focus group or individual TA discussion
Questionnaire	Learner views	Complete with individual learners or groups
	Family views	Ask families to complete
	Teacher reflections	Termly staff meeting completion
	TA reflections	Ask TAs to complete termly
Content analysis	APDR analysis	Schedule for use when reviewing sample APDRs

Learning Support Walk

Context: Date:
Completed by:

Information requested by:

Purpose/theme:

Anticipated impact:

Actual impact:

Observation summary (notes overleaf)

Positives:

Areas to develop:

Action required:

SEN Information Report – Practical Application

Date: Completed by:

Extract from SEN Information Report to be reviewed:

What I hope to see …

What I actually saw …

Strengths

Areas for development

Implications for action

Learner Engagement Observation Schedule

Pupil:
Class:

Date:
Staff Present:

Focus/theme/observation question:

Observation notes:

Points to clarify:

Strengths:

Areas for development:

Information to feedback:

Learner Evaluation – Interview Schedule

Pupil: Date:
Class: Staff present:

Focus/theme/observation question:

Do you like being at school?

What are you good at?

Is anything feeling tricky or challenging?

Does anything or anyone help with this?

What are you trying to learn or get better at?

Is there anything that you would change about your class?

Is there anything else you want to say about your time in school?

Family Consultation – Interview Schedule

Meeting with: Date:
Learner name: Class/year group:

Focus:

How do you think your child is getting on at school?

Do they like school?

What are they good at?

Are they finding anything tricky or challenging?

Is anything or anyone helping with this?

Do you feel informed about their learning strengths and barriers?

Do you feel listened to?

Is there anything you would like to change?

Teacher Evaluation – Interview Schedule

Meeting with: Date:

Class/year group:

Focus/theme:

How many learners in your class(es) have SEND?

What are some of the barriers to learning that are presented?

How do you overcome or try to remove these barriers?

What is working well?

What is more challenging?

How useful is the assess, plan, do and review process?

Do you need more training or support?

What would this look like?

TA Evaluation – Interview Schedule

Meeting with: Date:

Class/year group:

Focus/theme:

Tell me about your role …

What is working well?

What is more challenging?

Do you have time to collaborate with your teacher(s)?

Do you need more training or support?

What would this look like?

Learner Questionnaire

Thank you for agreeing to answer these questions. Your answers will help us to think about what is working well at school and anything that needs to improve.

Do you like being at school?	Yes	No	Sometimes
Do you have friends at school?	Yes	No	Sometimes
Do you understand your work?	Yes	No	Sometimes
Do you need help to do your work?	Yes	No	Sometimes
Do adults help you with your work?	Yes	No	Sometimes
Do you know what you are good at?	Yes	No	Sometimes
Do you know what you are trying to get better at?	Yes	No	Sometimes
Have you seen your learning plan?	Yes	No	Sometimes
Are you good at learning?	Yes	No	Sometimes
Do you find learning tricky?	Yes	No	Sometimes
Are you confident as a learner?	Yes	No	Sometimes
Does your teacher think you are good at learning?	Yes	No	Sometimes
Do your family think you are good at learning?	Yes	No	Sometimes
Would you like to be in a different class?	Yes	No	Sometimes
Do you like play and lunchtimes?	Yes	No	Sometimes

Family Questionnaire

Thank you for agreeing to answer these questions. Your answers will help us to think about what is working well at school and anything that needs to improve.

Does your child like being at school?	Yes	No	Sometimes
Do they have friends at school?	Yes	No	Sometimes
Do they understand their work?	Yes	No	Sometimes
Do they need help to do their work?	Yes	No	Sometimes
Do they get the help they need?	Yes	No	Sometimes
Do they tell you what they are good at?	Yes	No	Sometimes
Do you know what they are trying to get better at?	Yes	No	Sometimes
Have you seen their learning plan?	Yes	No	Sometimes
Were you involved in writing their plan?	Yes	No	Sometimes
Do they find learning tricky?	Yes	No	Sometimes
Are they confident as a learner?	Yes	No	Sometimes
Does their teacher think they are good at learning?	Yes	No	Sometimes
Do you think they are good at learning?	Yes	No	Sometimes
Would you like them to be in a different class?	Yes	No	Sometimes
Do they like play and lunchtimes?	Yes	No	Sometimes

Teacher Questionnaire

Thank you for agreeing to answer these questions. Your answers will help us to think about what is working well at school and anything that needs to improve.

Do you like teaching here?	Yes	No	Sometimes
Do you feel valued and listened to?	Yes	No	Sometimes
Is the workload manageable?	Yes	No	Sometimes
Do you have resources to adapt teaching?	Yes	No	Sometimes
Are you confident about teaching all learners?	Yes	No	Sometimes
Would you like more training on SEND?	Yes	No	Sometimes
Have your CPD needs been met?	Yes	No	Sometimes
Do learners with SEND make good progress?	Yes	No	Sometimes
Are you confident in holding SEN support meetings?	Yes	No	Sometimes
Do you use learner EHCPs?	Yes	No	Sometimes
Do you get support from the SENCO?	Yes	No	Sometimes
Can you use TA time to improve learning?	Yes	No	Sometimes
Are you confident to meet with families?	Yes	No	Sometimes
Is adult and child health and well-being a priority?	Yes	No	Sometimes
Do you feel supported in your role?	Yes	No	Sometimes

TA Questionnaire

Thank you for agreeing to answer these questions. Your answers will help us to think about what is working well at school and anything that needs to improve.

Do you like working here?	Yes	No	Sometimes
Do you feel valued and listened to?	Yes	No	Sometimes
Is the workload manageable?	Yes	No	Sometimes
Do you have the resources to do your job?	Yes	No	Sometimes
Are you confident about supporting all learners?	Yes	No	Sometimes
Would you like more training on SEND?	Yes	No	Sometimes
Have your CPD needs been met?	Yes	No	Sometimes
Do learners with SEND make good progress?	Yes	No	Sometimes
Do you use learning support plans?	Yes	No	Sometimes
Do you see learner EHCPs?	Yes	No	Sometimes
Do you get support from the SENCO?	Yes	No	Sometimes
Do you have time to talk to teachers?	Yes	No	Sometimes
Are you confident in your role?	Yes	No	Sometimes
Is adult and child health and well-being a priority?	Yes	No	Sometimes
Do you feel supported in your role?	Yes	No	Sometimes

APDR Analysis

Learner: **Class/year group:**
Date completed:

Is there evidence of …
Background Information?

Learner strengths?

Barriers to learning?

Are targeted outcomes SMART and relevant to need?

Is there detailed information about:
A – Area for development
B – Baseline information
C – Change anticipated
D – Do

Are learner views included?
Are family views included?
Is there a review date?

Is there a summary for the learner to use?
Is there evidence of progress?

Have targeted outcomes been carried forward?

Professional Evaluation

2. Create a QA task list

The ability to create lists is an essential skill for any SENCO or SEN Practitioner, but this particular list relates to the identification of strategic quality assurance tasks. It could be informed by some of the content of the QA Toolkit along with other ideas and activities that you would find useful. For some of you, this task may feel like writing a 'wish-list' rather than a realistic to-do list. Limited time and overstretched resources can reduce any sense of realism from such tasks. However, it is probably even more important to continue to aspire or 'wish' during demanding and challenging times as so often these wishes represent hopes or a belief in a different future. So, when time allows, do 'dare' to identify the QA and monitoring activities that you think would be most purposeful, even if you are not yet sure when they will be achieved.

As you begin this list, think about the strategic monitoring of the SEND system rather than the operational or individual learner-focused tasks that you complete. For example, rather than thinking about an individual parent meeting that is planned, consider activities that could provide feedback on parental confidence in the SEND system. Of course, you will continue to complete the individual parent meeting, but this is operational in focus and not strategic. Our operational activities do of course often 'reveal' the effectiveness or otherwise of our strategic systems and as the Educational Psychologist Tony Dessent once described, individual casework or operational activities can be considered rather like a 'litmus test' of our systems. But for this purpose, we are thinking specifically about strategic monitoring activities. This might include:

- Sampling the quality and relevance of SEN support plans
- Completing a themed learning support walk
- Monitoring the delivery of interventions by TAs
- Observation of TA mediation in classes
- Focus group with a sample of learners receiving SEN provision
- Telephone consultation with a sample of parents/carers of learners receiving SEN provision
- Review work samples of learners with SEND

The example SENCO QA Strategic Task List contains a list of tasks that can be used as a possible starting point. It is not a definitive list and it will only be useful if you adapt and personalise this according to your setting and priorities. But it can help to start the identification of such activities and it encourages triangulation of quality assurance tasks. Collecting a sample of 'lived experiences' from learners themselves, families, teachers and TAs as well as regular opportunities for observation of the SEND system in action will provide essential information that can help to inform the evaluation of the effectiveness of the SEND system.

SENCO QA Strategic Task List – Example

SENCOs and SEN Practitioners are encouraged to use sampling to gather and triangulate evidence using the SEND QA toolkit and other sources of information including:

- Learning Support Walks – themed observations looking for evidence of implementing approaches outlined in the SEN Information Report
- Work scrutiny – discuss work with learners and staff
- Pupil Focus Group – elicit pupil views on the impact and quality of provision
- Family views – elicit views from family members via phone consultations or focus group meetings
- Quality and relevance of 'About Me' plans (or other 'assess, plan, do and review' formats)
- Update and evaluate SEND profile information – record, provision map, intervention index
- Update and evaluate SEN Information Report
- Co-produce annual updates of the SEN Information Report with staff, governors, learners and family members
- Teacher coaching and lesson study
- SEND governor meeting
- Family forums
- Evaluation of SEN related data – progress, attendance, exclusion
- Governor report

3. Protect time within an annual strategic planner

Strategic monitoring and quality assurance can only be completed if time is protected for such activities. The suggestion here is to identify a weekly time slot for short but regular actions. For example, Tuesday morning before break or Thursday afternoon from 1–3 pm. Clearly this will depend on your individual pattern of work and for some of you, identifying and protecting strategic time will be easier said than done. If that is the case, it is essential that you notify other leaders of this reality, and the tasks are therefore distributed or assimilated into other monitoring tasks. Or discuss the possible targeted release of your time for the completion of QA and monitoring tasks as outlined in the annual strategic plan. Quality assurance of SEND systems can be completed by any senior leader although as the SENCO and/or SEN Practitioner, it will be far more effective if you commission these tasks as part of your deliberate leadership responsibilities.

When a weekly strategic time slot has been identified, create an annual strategic plan. This can be in any format but should include the protected weekly slot for each half term in the academic year. The template version of the SENCO Annual Strategic Plan provides a simple form that you can either adopt or adapt and the filled-out version that follows provides a worked example for consideration. The QA task list has been used to identify key tasks that will be completed and repeated at different intervals in the year. For example, in week 1 of every first half term, time is spent updating the SEN record, SEN Information Report, provision map and profile information which helps to clarify the SEND 'intent' as it updates who is identified as having SEN and what the provision offer looks like. In week 3 of every half term, QA observations are prioritised, but with different themes plotted during the year. There are tasks that may appear operational, such as reminding teachers to complete the graduated approach paperwork in week 2 of each 'A' half term, but they are included here as they have strategic intent, as they promote the intended action of others. Two weeks later, in week 4, a sample of teacher SEN support paperwork is quality assured for relevance and ambition. The repetitive nature of distributing tasks into specific weeks in specific half terms, secures activity intent. It is also a powerful way of demonstrating SENCO or SEN Practitioner awareness, ownership and leadership of strategic activities. The comments box can help to capture immediate thoughts or realities, including the risk of carry forward due to a diary change. Any comments should be written for you to aid your professional evaluation at the end of the term and indeed year. The final page can provide a valuable summary and evaluation which can be used to inform future planning. As with all resources, included in this book, the annual strategic planner is included as a starting point so even if this format is not for you, the principles may still resonate, and you can apply this to another format and achieve the same goal.

 # SENCO Annual Strategic Plan

Weekly protected strategic session:

Autumn term 1A

Week	Theme	Comments
1		
2		
3		
4		
5		
6		

Autumn term 1B

Week	Theme	Comments
1		
2		
3		
4		
5		
6		

Spring term 2A

Week	Theme	Comments
1		
2		
3		
4		
5		
6		

Spring term 2B

Week	Theme	Comments
1		
2		
3		
4		
5		
6		

Summer term 3A

Week	Theme	Comments
1		
2		
3		
4		
5		
6		

Summer term 3B

Week	Theme	Comments
1		
2		
3		
4		
5		
6		

Professional Evaluation – Termly Notes to Self

Autumn

Strengths	Areas for Development	Action Required

Spring

Strengths	Areas for Development	Action Required

Summer

Strengths	Areas for development	Action required …

SENCO annual strategic plan

Weekly protected strategic session: Thursday afternoon 1–3.30 pm

Autumn term 1A

Week	Theme	Comments
1	Update SEN record, provision map and SEN-D profile and upload to SEN Information Report. Audit of SEN intervention resources and equipment.	Completed ok, emailed request for update to school website, chase next week.
2	Remind teachers to complete 'about me' plans with pupils. Pupil observation – nominated by teachers.	Observation of JP in class 3, good discussion with teacher.
3	Quality assurance observations of sample of TAs delivering interventions focus: Cognition and learning interventions.	Not keen on our working memory games, must ask Trust for other activities.
4	Evaluation of sample of teacher-completed 'about me': assess, plan, do and review forms for pupils at SEN Support.	All completed but weakness with baseline information - take to SLT.
5	Case sampling – review pupil 'about me' form and complete work scrutiny – evidence of support. SEN Governor Termly Liaison Meeting.	Governor not able to attend, so wrote a summary of actions for next governor meeting.
6	Pupil Focus Group – sample of pupils completing intervention, elicit views on effectiveness and impact.	Lovely afternoon! Pupils enjoyed going out but not sure if they are applying back in class?

Autumn term 1B

Week	Theme	Comments
1	Teacher 'coaching' lesson study opportunity – work with colleague to complete lesson study.	
2	Learning Support Walk focus: 'i-spy' evidence of use of adjustments and resources in classrooms.	
3	Quality assurance observations of sample of TAs delivering interventions focus: Yr R, 1, 2.	
4	Parent/Carer Focus Group invite SEN Governor.	
5	Sample completed 'reviews' of 'about me documents'.	
6	Phone sample of parents/carers to elicit their views regarding pupil progress and recent SEN support review meeting with Teacher.	

Spring term 2A

Week	Theme	Comments
1	Update SEN record, provision map and SEN-D profile and upload to SEN Information Report.	
2	Remind teachers to complete 'about me' plans with pupils. Pupil observation – nominated by teachers.	
3	Quality assurance observations of sample of TAs delivering interventions focus: Communication and interaction interventions.	
4	Evaluation of sample of teacher-completed assess, plan, do and review forms for pupils at SEN Support.	
5	Case sampling – review pupil 'about me' form and complete work scrutiny – evidence of support. SEN Governor Termly Liaison Meeting.	
6	Pupil Focus Group – sample of pupils completing intervention, elicit views on effectiveness and impact.	

Spring term 2B

Week	Theme	Comments
1	Teacher 'coaching' lesson study opportunity – work with colleague to complete lesson study.	
2	Learning Support Walk focus: 'i-spy' – evidence of provision approaches listed in our SEN Information Report.	
3	Quality assurance observations of sample of TAs delivering interventions focus: Yr 3, 4, 5, 6.	
4	Parent/Carer Focus Group invite SEN Governor.	
5	Sample completed 'reviews' of 'about me' documents.	
6	Phone sample of parents/carers to elicit their views regarding pupil progress and recent SEN support review meeting with Teacher	

Summer term 3A

Week	Theme	Comments
1	Update SEN Record, provision map and SEN-D profile and upload to SEN Information Report.	
2	Evaluate transition priorities – pupils leaving and pupils receiving. Remind teachers to complete 'about me' plans with pupils.	
3	Quality assurance observations of sample of TAs delivering interventions focus: Social, emotional and mental health interventions.	
4	Evaluation of sample of teacher-completed assess, plan, do and review forms for pupils at SEN Support.	
5	Case sampling – review pupil 'about me' form and complete work scrutiny – evidence of support. SEN Governor Termly Liaison Meeting.	
6	Pupil Focus Group – sample of pupils completing intervention, elicit views on effectiveness and impact.	

Summer term 3B

Week	Theme	Comments
1	Teacher 'coaching' lesson study opportunity – work with colleague to complete lesson study.	
2	Learning Support Walk focus: 'i-spy' evidence of mediating questions used by adults with pupils	
3	Quality assurance observations of sample of TAs delivering interventions focus: Physical and sensory interventions.	
4	Parent/Carer Focus Group invite SEN Governor.	
5	Sample completed 'reviews' of 'about me' documents.	
6	Phone sample of parents/carers to elicit their views regarding pupil progress and recent SEN support review meeting with teacher.	

Professional evaluation – termly notes to self

Autumn

Strengths	Areas for Development	Action Required
Pupils are enjoying interventions and have good relationships with support staff. All 'About Me' forms completed by all Staff	TAs and teachers to make explicit the purpose of interventions and actively 'encourage' application in class. Quite weak on capturing baseline and starting point.	Discuss methods for capturing starting points with EP at next visit. Review 7 Cs progress tracker for baseline ideas.

Spring

Strengths	Areas for Development	Action Required

Summer

Strengths	Areas for Development	Action Required

4. Involve others

The involvement of others in SEND quality assurance is highly valuable and at the heart of effective SEND leadership as it promotes engagement and empowerment. Encouraging other senior leaders to undertake SEND-themed learning walks exploring the implementation of a specific topic will promote greater awareness and a shared culture and understanding of the importance of SEND. Similarly, supporting teachers to work together to write SEN Support plans and to review the quality and relevance of targeted outcomes will also promote learning and shared evaluation. Providing opportunities for TAs to rehearse or role-play mediated questions with each other, or to share the content of their learning support toolkit, providing the rationale and application of items, will also boost consistency and confidence, improving practice. Similarly, involving learners in the active evaluation of their SEND provision by ensuring their participation in SEN Support meetings and conversations about strengths and areas for development will aid the quality of their engagement in interviews and questionnaires. This is also true for their family members and our governors or trustees.

Collaboration is an essential tool for leadership and a useful starting point in your evaluation of strengths and areas for development within your setting. Where do you collaborate as a staff? Is this structured or unstructured? Is everyone involved? How involved are learners in their learning and/or SEND provision? Do you maximise opportunities for parental collaboration, or could more be done? Establish your own baseline and seek to consider any further opportunities for development.

5. Regularly feed back

Not only is it important for SENCOs and SEN Practitioners to complete sampled quality assurance activities, but it is also essential that this information is evaluated and shared with others. A summary of termly findings can be included in information shared with governors as well as senior leaders. It can be shared as updates in staff meetings or as a message on staff whiteboards, as well as being included within your SEN Information Report. Including a short commentary about QA findings and any actions arising from this will further evidence the relevance and responsiveness of your SEND systems and your commitment to pursuing your 'best endeavours'. **Remember to evaluate, and not just narrate your actions, as this evaluation is the difference between leading and coordinating. The job title for a SENCO may currently refer to coordination, but the job description is leadership.** When time allows, think about how information is shared with governors or trustees and reflect on the content of the template Report to Governers and the filled-out example for Willow School. Are there any headings or themes that could be added to your current system for governor communication?

 # SEND Report to Governors

Term

There should be a member of the governing body or a sub-committee with specific oversight of the school's arrangements for SEN and disability. School leaders should regularly review how expertise and resources used to address SEN can be used to build the quality of whole-school provision as part of their approach to school improvement.

(Code of Practice, 2015, page 92, paragraph 6.3)

SEN Profile – Who are our learners with SEN?

National =

Our school =

Year Group Distribution of Pupils at SEN Support

	Cognition and Learning	Communication and Interaction	Social, Emotional and Mental Health	Physical and or Sensory
Year				
Year				
Year				
Total				

Currently, the majority of pupils at SEN Support require support for:

The number of boys with SEN is:
The number of girls with SEN is:

The following pupils have SEN and are also represented in another group:
LAC   EAL   Traveller   Disabled   Pupil Premium

The number of pupils with SEN receiving exclusions this term is:
The number of pupils with SEN with persistent absence concerns is:

Actions taken:

The number of disabled pupils in school is:
The number of pupils with medical needs is:

SEN Provision – What do we offer our learners with SEN?

Our provision map and SEN Information Report:

Impact of Provision – What difference are we making to learners with SEN?

SENCO views:

What teachers have said:

What parents/carers have said:

What pupils have said:

SENCO Evaluation of Provision and Next Steps

Whole-school Implications

SEN CPD and Impact

SENCO:

What:

Impact:

Whole school:

What:

Impact:

Request to Governors:

Signed:
Date:

Willow School SEN Report to Governors – Example

Autumn term 2024

There should be a member of the governing body or a sub-committee with specific oversight of the school's arrangements for SEN and disability. School leaders should regularly review how expertise and resources used to address SEN can be used to build the quality of whole-school provision as part of their approach to school improvement.

(Code of Practice 2015, page 92, paragraph 6.3)

SEN Profile – Who are our learners with SEN?

15.2% of pupils (38/250 children) at Willow School are identified as having SEN; nationally, this figure is 18.4%

Of these, 2.4% (6/250 children) have an Education, Health and Care Plan (EHCP); national is 4.8%

12.8% (32/250 children) are at SEN support; national is 13.6%

Year Group Distribution of Pupils at SEN Support

	Cognition and Learning	Communication and Interaction	Social, Emotional and Mental Health	Physical and or Sensory
Year R, 1 and 2	4	3		
Year 3 and 4	5	4	3	
Year 5 and 6	3	3	4	3
Total	12	10	7	3

Currently, the majority of pupils at SEN Support require support for cognition and learning and communication and interaction.

The number of boys with SEN is: 25
The number of girls with SEN is: 13

The following pupils have SEN and are also represented in another group:
LAC = 2   EAL   Traveller   Disabled   Pupil Premium = 20

The number of pupils with **SEN receiving exclusions** this term is: 0
The number of pupils with **SEN with persistent absence** concerns is: 2

Actions taken:
- SMT monitoring and liaison with parents

The number of disabled pupils in school is: 7
The number of pupils with medical needs is: 3

SEN Provision – What do we offer our learners with SEN?

The attached provision map outlines the provision that is 'additional to or different from' the differentiated curriculum. This is funded from our SEN budget, which this year is a total of £55,000. The majority of our budget is spent on employing additional adults to support and deliver targeted intervention. This term's monitoring activity of the deployment of additional adults found that

30% of Additional Adult time was spent on **mediation** tasks in class.
20% of Additional Adult time was spent on **reinforcement** tasks.
35% of Additional Adult time was spent on **intervention** activities.
15% of Additional Adult time was spent on **assessment** activities.

Impact of Provision – What difference are we making to learners with SEN?

SENCO views:
- Individual learning profiles suggest good progress towards targets.
- Working memory intervention is popular and valued by staff and pupils
- Increasing concerns about expressive vocabulary and writing

What teachers have said:
- Additional support for writing requested
- Working memory intervention is popular with pupils

What parents/carers have said:

My daughter really enjoys the literacy group with Mrs Jones and I think her reading is improving.

J showed me his 'About Me' sheet and is excited about learning his words.

What pupils have said:

I like working with Mr Fraser I can do the work.

I like nurture we get to make toast.

SENCO Evaluation of Provision and Next Steps

This term we have introduced a working memory activity group in Key Stage 1 and 2 to target the development of pupils at SEN Support for Cognition and Learning. This has been very popular with pupils and parents/carers. Teachers have also adopted whole-class prompts to support pupils in class. This will continue into next term. The daily reading buddy group will also continue, although it has been agreed that this will form part of an adult-supervised reading session, so follow-up questions can be asked of pairs. This will help to ensure that buddies focus on reading and do not become distracted. Further consideration will be given to developing expressive vocabulary and the link with writing.

Whole-school Implications

Writing continues to be an area for targeted development and fits with the need to increase expressive vocabulary across the school. Recent whole-school training on mental health services was useful and senior leaders are considering the use of PATHS.

SEN CPD and Impact

SENCO: Termly Essential SENCO Network meeting focused on national news, including imminent changes to SEND system and future revised code of practice. Two CPD taster sessions: liaison with governors and metacognition.

Impact: New report format used for feeding back to governors. Metacognition information to be shared with staff at meeting in January.

Whole school:
- 2 TAs continue with ELSA training
- All staff mental health training

Impact: Feedback was positive, but too early to implement, will be monitored during the term.

Request to Governors:
- Promote participation in SEN Information Report working party with parents at every opportunity! Particularly at Christmas fete.

Signed:

Date:

Quality assurance

The purpose of this chapter has been to promote the opportunities of quality assurance tasks and to break them into short and manageable activities that can be assimilated into a year. Little but often is the key, along with purpose and relevance. Integrating tasks in this way will ensure that you can robustly 'test' the systems that you lead and help you to evaluate and evolve next steps.

> **Reflections**
>
> - Is there a weekly or fortnightly time slot that could be protected for quality assurance tasks?
> - Who else is carrying out regular quality assurance tasks and are there opportunities for them to adopt an SEND theme or focus?
> - Can you adopt or adapt any of the templates to help capture your QA tasks?
> - Have you defined the type of QA tasks you want to complete or delegate to others?
> - What opportunities exist for you to provide feedback your findings?

> **Actions to consider**
>
> - Protect some time to write a QA monitoring task list and attempt to plot some of these tasks into the annual strategic planner.
> - Discuss QA and monitoring with other senior leaders and share your QA monitoring task list. Identify any opportunities in existing monitoring sessions where other leaders could complete tasks and share findings.
> - Review the SEND QA Toolkit and identify resources that immediately resonate and feel useful, then start with these.

4. Intent

Clarity and shared understanding regarding the intent of SEND identification and provision are at the heart of effective SEND leadership. Indeed, clarity and shared understanding of intent are also central to learning. Within Book 2, *SEND Intervention: Planning Provision with Purpose*, we explored the 4 Functions of Learning Support, which is a framework for the deployment of teaching assistants (TAs). If you are familiar with this, you will recall that mediation is the first of the 4 Functions, along with reinforcement of a skill and or learning behaviour, assessment and intervention. Mediation as a term was selected because of its theoretical origins to the concept of a 'mediated learning experience' (MLE) introduced by Reuven Feuerstein. As the Mediation Process Prompt shows, Feuerstein argued that an MLE requires intent, reciprocity, meaning and transcendence, and it is these factors that make it distinct from other shared learning opportunities, including play-based learning. Defining the intent of what is to be learnt, along with the acquisition of reciprocity or agreement from the learner, who shares the meaning and potential for application, is what defines this.

DOI: 10.4324/9781003408994-5

Mediation process prompt

A mediated learning experience must contain …

Intentionality	Reciprocity	Meaning	Transcendence
The learning activity must have a clear purpose and intent	The learning process is shared, the learner must want to engage	The activity must have a defined meaning and purpose for the learner	The learning should be relevant and be able to be applied in other contexts
This is what we are doing …	We are doing this together	This is why we are doing this …	This is how you can use this another time

Knowing the purpose and anticipated impact of SEND identification and provision is the first step in its fruition. I wonder though whether time allows us to define our intent? Often, time is so limited, and we are aware of the need to do things so we embark on implementation without protecting time to explore intent. Take a moment to consider the following three questions:

- What is the purpose of identifying a learner as having SEND?
- What do you expect will be different for them as a result of this?
- What do you want staff to do to support learners with SEND?

Now take a moment to consider the SEND system that you are managing or have created.

- What is the purpose of SEND paperwork*? (*paperwork is used here as a general term and includes electronic information and not just paper.)
- Who writes it, reads it and actually uses it?
- Why do *you* 'assess, plan, do and review'? Is it because the Code of Practice 2015 defines this as a requirement, or because your Local Authority require you to evidence-base actions? Or is it because it gives you meaningful information to support the planning of next steps for learners with SEND?

Now think of some of the learners that are identified as having SEND …

- In what way do you expect their lived experience in your setting to change as a result of the SEND system that you are leading?
- How do you want them to feel about themselves?
- What do you want to be different for them by the end of the next half term?

These questions have been written to illustrate the purpose or the intent of SEND identification and to help you define the anticipated impact of your SEND system. Those of you familiar with books one and two from this trilogy will know that I refer to the two AA words, 'anticipated' and 'actual', with regards to capturing impact. If we define what we hope or anticipate will be different, then it is easier to measure whether this has been achieved. **So, keep in mind, what is your anticipated intent for the SEND system that you lead? And where have you defined this?**

SEN Information Report and SEN policy

The Code of Practice 2015 includes the requirement for all settings to publish an SEN Information Report. This is the setting's contribution to the local offer and is intended to provide a one-stop shop or overview of the systems for SEND identification and provision. In fact, the Code includes a list of 14 bullet points as requirements, each of which has its own merit and purpose, but collectively, these requirements risk detracting from the initial intention of the report. The original purpose of the SEN Information Report was to provide key information for families. Ironically, schools and settings that comply with all 14 bullet points often create a document that becomes less accessible to families because of the sheer volume of content! Instead of being the intended 'shop window' showcasing all that is available for learners with SEND, the SEN Information Report can feel more like a 'warehouse', which is far harder to navigate or relate to. This is a poignant example of how the intent of something was positive, but the required implementation reduced the fulfilment of the intent. It will be interesting to see in the years ahead whether revisions to the Code of Practice 2015 address this issue by retaining the intent of the SEN Information Report as a tool for families with consideration to the accessibility of the content, or in fact, redefine the intent in terms of SEND accountability? Within your role, it may be interesting to review *who* actually reads the SEN Information Report in your setting? My professional experience is that the report is predominantly read by professional visitors to the setting, including Ofsted and Trust or LA officers, rather than families themselves.

A related question to consider around the SEN Information Report is: how often do you, as the SENCO or SEN Practitioner, read your report and, importantly, your SEN policy? After all, if the SEN Information Report is your published 'shop window', then the intent of your SEN policy is to provide the 'how-to' guide or staff handbook regarding SEN implementation. But who reads and uses the SEN policy, or indeed any of our setting policies? There are times when I have read a policy, got to the end and genuinely had no idea what I had just read! I certainly couldn't deduce what the implications were for practice. I often wonder whether there is a specific filter or language that we use when writing policies that doesn't seem to translate into the real world! Yet a policy has such potential for capturing and defining intent and thus by implication shaping implementation. But are we fulfilling this potential?

Evidence of fulfilled potential in this context is whether the documents are actually used. Do you know how many teachers directly *use* the SEN policy as a reference point or guide? Do you know many staff members who have read the SEN Information Report to gain an insight into the SEN system in your setting? How many parents have commented on the SEN Information Report? And how often do *you* use either of these documents within your work? The SEN Information Report itself can help to inform your quality assurance strategy. You can 'check out' whether what is written in the Information Report is actually visible in classes using one of the tools within the SEND QA Toolkit from Chapter 3. This can be particularly useful as ironically, you may face greater criticism for claiming to do something in your SEN Information Report and not delivering on this, than for not writing it in the first place! Similarly, what is written in your policy should be evidence based. But how often do leaders look for that evidence? We spend vast amounts of time creating these documents but then forget to use them within our own work. The compliance checklist below could be a useful prompt to aid your evaluation of the settings SEN Information Report. There are also a set of questions that governors could use when exploring the SEN Information Report. If they can answer the questions, this suggests compliance with the required elements of the SEN Information Report.

Is your SEN Information Report compliant?

- The SEN Information Report is a statutory requirement.
- All schools and settings must publish an updated SEN Information Report annually.
- It is the school's contribution to the local offer.
- It is an SEN Information Report – not an SEN-**D** Information Report. The adaptions offered to disabled learners should be explicit within the school's access plan.

To be compliant the SEN Information Report **must** describe:

- The range of SEN provided for in the school that year
- How SEN is identified, the types of assessments used, and the name and contact details of the SENCO
- How the school engages with parents and children with SEN and involves them in their child's education
- How children and young people are consulted about their own learning
- How progress and outcomes are monitored and assessed, including the engagement of parents and children in this review
- How children are supported to move between phases of education and in to adulthood
- The school's approach to teaching children and young people with SEN
- How the curriculum and learning environment is adapted for learners with SEN
- The expertise and training of staff to support children with SEN, including how specialist expertise is accessed when required
- How the school evaluates the effectiveness of provision
- How children with SEN are enabled to engage in activities alongside their peers who do not have SEN
- How the school supports the improvement of emotional and social development of learners with SEN, including how it listens to the views of children and prevents bullying
- How the school involves other agencies in meeting the needs of children with SEN and supporting their families
- What are the arrangements for handling complaints from parents of children with SEN relating to the provision offered by the school

Questions to explore compliance of the SEN Information Report

To 'test' the compliance of your SEN Information Report, read your report and try and answer these questions:

1. What percentage of learners in the school have been identified with SEN?
2. What are the types of barriers to learning experienced by children with SEN in the school?
3. What assessments are used in the school?
4. How does the school involve children and families in planning and reviewing learning?
5. How are children supported through transitions on to their next phase of education or prepared for adulthood?
6. What is the schools approach to teaching children with SEN?
7. How does the school adapt curriculum and learning environment to support those with SEN?
8. What training in SEN have school staff completed or plan to complete?
9. Does the school have support from SEN specialists?
10. How does the school know if SEN provision is effective?
11. What activities are available for all children in the school?
12. How does the school listen to the views of children and young people?
13. What does the school do to prevent bullying and promote friendships and social skills?
14. How does the school access support for families from the LA, health and voluntary/other services?
15. Is it clear how parents could complain about the provision offered for children with SEN, and what the procedures are?
16. How do you know when this was written, and when it will be reviewed?
17. How could you offer feedback on this report or take part in the review?

When time allows, re-read your SEN Information Report and your SEN policy and consider the following:

- Is the intent of your policy and processes for SEND explicit?
- Do you know what this would look like in practice?
- Have you seen this in practice?

If the answer to any of these questions is 'no' or 'not really', then consider how this could be refined. Integrating the use of the SEN Information Report within your quality assurance work will help to ensure relevance of the report itself and inform your evaluation of the effectiveness of your systems. Intent is not only written in these documents; it can also be evidenced within our curriculum plans, relationship and/or behavioural policies, our access plan and even information about clubs and activities. Intent refers to our desired outcomes or purpose and reminds us that as part of the process of provision mapping (not just the generation of our provision map), we should be defining our expectations or anticipated impact. Provision mapping is a management tool that encourages reflection on resources, needs, planning, delivery and review. It is the ultimate leaders' assess, plan, do and review cycle! The SEND Intent Self-Evaluation comprises a self-review form that may help you to explore and formulate your SEND intent.
At first glance, it may appear long-winded and wordy, but the strength of the document is the thinking that is stimulates rather than the words that are recorded. So even if you use the questions to scaffold a leadership conversation about intent, and record only saliant points, the process itself should be useful. And if not, as always, please adapt or adopt this starting point and create a better fit for yourself and your context.

SEND Intent Self-Evaluation

The purpose of these questions is to encourage reflection on your intent for the SEND system. Use the questions to scaffold your thinking and to remind yourself of the purpose of SEND identification and provision.

- Why do you identify a learner as having SEN(D)?

- What do you anticipate will be different as a result of this?

- How do you identify strengths and barriers to learning?

- How do you identify next steps and or targeted outcomes?

- Who is involved in this process? Would you like to involve anyone else?

- What is the purpose of SEN provision?

- Is this view shared by staff, leaders, learners and their families?

- Does the SEN Information Report capture your intent for the SEN system? If not, what is does it capture?

- Are learners and their families aware of the intent of their learning plans and provision that is additional to or different from the adapted curriculum?

- How would you know if the SEND system is effective in supporting learners?

Intent can also be viewed within our SEN provision, both in terms of the principles underpinning our adjustments, the types of support and resources we make available to learners with SEND and of course in our approach to learner engagement with interventions. If we adopt a person-centred approach to SEND provision, then the learner is at the heart of our actions. Adjustments will be relevant to learner need but also will promote ownership, empowerment and independence. Similarly, if we teach learners to choose and select resources and to request targeted support, they retain control, engagement and are less likely to experience low self efficacy or learned-helplessness or passivity as a consequence of our provision. Similarly, if we invite learners to participate with interventions and explain the purpose of engagement and the anticipated outcome of their participation, then they will have a greater sense of application and generalisation. Rather than just having a 'nice' time in a small, safe setting, they have clarity of purpose and are reminded of the specific skills that are being taught and that they can rehearse and apply in the classroom. Intent is a far reaching, non-negotiable requirement of SEND leadership for SENCOs and SEN Practitioners, and for our class and subject teachers and TAs working with groups of learners with SEND.

SEND intent and attainment

The intent of a SEND system is multi-faceted in the same way as the intent of the education system itself is. Of course, the purpose of education is to educate by sharing knowledge of a curriculum, teaching skills and boosting attainment, but it is also about achievement and personal development. It is about motivation, aspiration, communication, interaction, reflection, self-regulation, curiosity and discovery. Similarly, the intent of the SEND system is to advance attainment progress relative to starting points, but it is also about personalised progress and achievement. So often our vocabulary in education focuses solely on curriculum attainment. And although this is an essential element of shared intent, we should also be monitoring personalised progress and achievement. For a learner with SEND, personalised progress may relate to targeted outcomes or the achievement of targets on learning plans and or an Education, Health and Care Plan (EHCP). Achievements could relate to participation in a group or an activity club or feeling safe and secure to arrive in school or stay in the classroom. It could be learning to swim or ride a bike or any other sport or craft interest or activity. But where do we capture and report this? So often, when we are asked to demonstrate progress, the focus shifts solely to curriculum attainment. And yes, this is a vital element, but for learners with SEND, we should also be capturing the intent, implementation and impact of their SEND provision.

SEND provision is defined as our 'action with intent' and can be considered as a balance between adjustments, support/resources and interventions. The intent of adjustments, support and resources is often to overcome barriers to learning and to enable participation and access to the adapted curriculum. The intent of intervention is to teach or refine a specific skill that may, if possible, 'remove' the barrier to learning. Of course, not all barriers can or should be removed, but with regards to skill acquisition and or refinement this can be a highly relevant intent of an intervention. Teachers can define the intent of an intervention within a letter to a learner, where they are invited to take part in an intervention as is demonstrated in the letter to Anita that follows. An invitation, not only establishes the components of a mediated learning experience, i.e. it defines intent, provides an opportunity for reciprocity and explains meaning and transcendence, but it also means adults and learners have a shared understanding of intent or purpose of the intervention. Writing a bank of intervention letters can appear time consuming for one member of staff, but if time is made available during a staff meeting, each member of staff could write one, two or three letters, thus creating a bank of letters that can be personalised for individual learners.

Defining intent does not have to be excessively time consuming, but it does require thinking time. The following development plan prompt could be useful in helping you to protect time to define and refine the annual intent of your SEND systems. Again, it is offered as a starting point, and you may choose to complete some of the headings rather than all, as long as the process stimulates thinking and reflection and helps you to develop clarity of intent, as this will help you in your leadership of its implementation.

Learner Invitation

Dear Anita,

You are invited to take part in an activity group with three other children. The group will meet every week for four weeks to take part in a series of games that will last about 20 minutes. The games are chosen to help you think of words and feelings. I have noticed that sometimes it is hard for you to think of the words to say to share how you are feeling. I hope that by playing these games you will be able to use words to describe your feelings.

If you have any questions about this please do ask me, but I hope you will enjoy taking part with this group and it helps you to talk about feelings.

Keep working hard!

Best wishes

Ms Carter

SEND Development Plan

Year:

About us, our school context:

Our learners:

Our families:

Our staff:

Our SENCO:

Our SLT:

Our Governors:

Whole school development priorities:

Strengths of SEND identification and provision:

Areas for development:

Targeted outcomes for the year ahead

1.

2.

3.

4.

5.

6.

Anticipated impact:

Actual impact:

End of year evaluation:

SEND development plan Willow Tree Primary Academy

Year: 2024–2025

About us, our school context:
Willow Tree Primary Academy has 295 pupils on its roll. We are based in a rural community seven miles outside of Norwich. We have 14% of learners identified as having SEN with 3% having an EHCP. We have 35% of learners who receive Pupil Premium and 10% of learners are Looked After. 20% of learners have English as a second language. The school was built in 1982 and four classes are open plan. There is a playground and a small field.

Our learners:
11% of learners are supported at SEN support. With 5% for communication and interaction, 3% cognition and learning, 2% social, emotional and mental health and 1% physical and sensory.

Our families:
We have good attendance at Parents' Evening but less engagement with questionnaires and SEND focus groups.

Our staff:
Ten FTE teachers, 13 TAs who make ten FTE. Six FTE TAs work across year groups 1–6, two in reception and two Intervention Leads. Six MDAs. Access to Play Therapist, EP and SALT.

Our SENCO:
SENCO completed the National Award in 2017. Ongoing training via Essential SENCO Network and member of NASEN. Additional training in ELKLAN, ELSA and dyslexia level 7.

Our SLT:
Five members of SLT: Head, Deputy, two Assistant Heads and SENCO

Our Governors:
Seven members of the governing body. Named SEN governor who meets with SENCO termly. SENCO writes termly updates on SEND for governor meetings.

Whole-school development priorities:
Writing and Feedback have been key priorities for 2023–2024 along with review of curriculum connectedness for disadvantaged learners.

Strengths of SEND identification and provision:

1. Alternative means of recording – staff now use a range of recording methods in classes including, voice recorder, typing, filming and peer scribes.
2. Staff know their children – fundamental to our principles is knowledge of our children. There is good communication between adults and children throughout the school.
3. Parental/carer confidence – there continues to be no formal complaints from families of children with SEND and those that completed the questionnaire were confident in the provision offered.

Areas for development:

1. The quality and diversity of SEN support – analysis of learning support passports revealed a limited range of targets all tending to be curriculum based. We are going to provide training on the 7 Cs Learning Portfolio to increase the quality and diversity of provision offered at SEN Support.
2. Speech and Language in the Early Years – we need to review the language that is modelled by adults in reception and year 1, to promote greater questioning and reflection as well as to extend vocabulary.
3. Writing relevant and SMART targeted outcomes.
4. Autism training for midday assistants and TAs.

5. Teacher adjustments to support learners with small working memory capacity.
6. SENCO quality assurance tasks – protect weekly time to complete regular sample of actions outlined in strategic planner.

Targeted outcomes for the year ahead

1. All teachers will use the language of the 7 Cs Learning Portfolio within their SEN support meetings with children and families SO THERE is a shared understanding of three strengths and three areas for development.
2. All Key Stage 1 staff will complete 'creating a communication culture' training with a speech therapist SO THEY can extend expressive and receptive vocabulary within play with children.
3. All teachers will attend staff training on targeted outcomes SO THEY can write relevant targets within SEN support plans that connect the action (intent) with the impact.
4. All midday assistants and TAs will complete the face to face introduction to autism training SO THEY feel more confident to respond to the individual needs of learners during lunchtime.
5. All teachers will read *Working Memory in the Classroom* by Gathercole and Alloway and identify key actions to reduce memory load when teaching SO THEY can make adjustments when teaching.
6. SENCO to identify a core list of quality assurance activities and plot these throughout the year using the annual strategic planner SO THEY can confidently 'test out' SEND systems and provisions in place to inform adjustments and next steps.

Anticipated impact:

1. Teachers will feel more confident to complete SEN support meetings and parents/carers and learners will feel more engaged.
2. Adults will model a range of questions and key words during play activities with children who will then be able to replicate these words themselves.
3. Higher quality and greater relevance of SEND targeted outcomes, so teachers, learners and families have greater awareness of what they are working on. This will also mean that impact can be measured more clearly.

4. Less negative incidents at play and lunchtimes between staff and learners with autism. More structured play tasks and positive interactions between staff and learners with autism.
5. Greater knowledge and understanding amongst teachers about what working memory is and how they can try to reduce the memory load for learners in their lessons.
6. SENCO to feel more confident and assured by the evidence base of impact of SEND provision as well as the schools approach to implementation.

Actual impact:

1. Positive response to 7 Cs Learning Portfolio with staff now feeling far more confident – can't remember not using it!
2. Great start with language development but found questioning became too complex so focused more on vocabulary in play.
3. Targeted outcomes far more relevant and meaningful – great response from staff and parents.
4. Training went well but more has been requested, particularly regarding responding to behaviour.
5. Training was valued but still quite hard to do. Mixed response to implementation, will need to develop this further.
6. Great start with strategic tasks, but only achieved 70% of plan, but this was very useful and insightful and will help to structure future steps.

End of year evaluation:

Overall a good year for SEND development with lots achieved. Intent, matched implementation resulting in positive impact. Lots to still do but good ending to this year, leads to good beginning!

The intent of the 7 Cs Learning Portfolio

Those of you who have adopted the 7 Cs Learning Portfolio as part of your language of SEND assessment and provision also need to remain mindful of the intent of this strengths-based approach. At the start of any initiative there is clarity of purpose and shared anticipated outcomes but as time passes, the intent can become 'assumed' as it is simply something that is 'done'. For those involved in the initiative from the beginning this can be a positive as it demonstrates an internalised assimilation of a way of working, but as we know in education, staff members change and it is essential that we continue to make explicit the implicit of our systems for the benefit of new and existing colleagues.

- So what is your intent for using the 7 Cs Learning Portfolio?
- How would you describe this?
- Has it changed and evolved over time?

As the author, my intent of writing the 7 Cs was to provide a language of SEND assessment, in particular of SEN Support. It was to aid teacher assessment with the identification of strengths and areas for development and to help define provision that is 'additional to or different from' the adapted curriculum offer, boosting the quality, relevance and diversity of SEN Support and avoiding 'more of the same'. A strengths-based language in turn was intended to promote clarity, consistency and a shared understanding between staff, learners and their families, increasing communication and confidence of all. But what was your intent for adopting this approach, or if you are beginning to consider the 7 Cs Learning Portfolio, consider why you might choose to do this?

Vicki McClure, SENCO at Pulham Primary school in Norfolk, described their intent for using the 7 Cs in relation to support plans. She writes:

> We have used the 7 Cs approach for the first time this year to inform our support plans. They have transformed how all staff approach the barriers that children face by focusing on strengths rather than weaknesses. It has sharpened our target setting and definitely improved our practise.

Hannah Powley, Early Years SENCO at St. Nicholas Priory CEVA Primary School, reports:

> At St. Nicholas we have been using the 7 Cs for a number of years as we wanted a framework that could better celebrate our learners with SEND,

without purely focusing on attainment. Initially it was to support the whole school staff with the language used to support our learners with SEND when writing learning plans. However as time has progressed we have been able to implement the assessment framework across the whole school. Now all learning plans have integrated progress measures relating to the 7 Cs framework that can show clear progress for individuals. Our specialist unit has been using this assessment framework for some time and we were able to present some excellent progress data for our children with the most complex needs during a recent inspection. The 7 Cs has transformed our whole school SEND approach.

The purpose, or indeed intent, of this chapter, is to explicitly promote the importance of the 'why' stage of our thinking and actions particularly with regards to SEND identification and provision. **As a leader of the SEND system, it is essential that you have clarity of purpose as this will either underpin or undermine all that you do.**

Reflections

- What is the intent of your SEND system?
- Is this shared and understood by others?
- Where is this written?
- How is it shared?
- Are you using this intent, to aid your quality assurance and monitoring of the implementation and impact of SEND provision?

Actions to consider

- Read your SEN Information Report and complete the compliance checklist, share the questions with governors and ask for their engagement and feedback.
- Look at the SEND development plan form and consider relevance for your setting.
- If you have adopted the 7 Cs Learning Portfolio in your setting, take time to review the impact. Consider the intent at the time of introduction and whether this has now changed or evolved?

5. Implementation

Evaluating the implementation of SEND systems is an essential role of leaders. It does, after all, involve exploring the daily lived experience of learners with SEND and staff working with them. But as discussed in Chapter 4, to do this there must be clarity regarding the intent of the systems. For example, if I am identified as requiring SEN support, what difference does that actually make? Is my name simply added to the SEN record, or does something 'additional to or different from' happen to me? Of course, we know that the national expectation is that learners identified as requiring SEN support should receive support that is 'additional to or different from' that readily available to learners of the same age, but in real terms what does that look like? And what if I have an Education, Health and Care Plan (EHCP), how does this influence my adapted curriculum and SEN provision offer? Many SENCOs and SEN Practitioners work tirelessly to define such provision and record it on a provision map, learning plan or passport, but the question remains … in real terms, how does this impact the learner on a daily basis?

There is a risk that for some learners, SEN support simply becomes 'more of the same'. For example, if a learner is identified as having a difficulty with maths, then they receive more maths. Of course, they should receive more maths, planned relative to their starting point, but this is their curriculum offer; it is not SEN support that is 'additional to or different from'. Those of you familiar with the 7 Cs Learning Portfolio will know that the 7 Cs attempt to provide a language of SEND assessment and help to define 'additional to or different from'. So, for the learner who is struggling with maths, they receive more maths as part of their adapted curriculum offer, but as they are identified as having SEN and in need of SEN support, the 7 Cs can help staff, families and the learner themselves identify potential barriers to learning that are impacting their access to maths. This could include working memory, speed of processing, language or attention and impulsivity. Action to either overcome or, if possible, to remove these barriers is then instigated as the SEN Support that is additional to or different from.

DOI: 10.4324/9781003408994-6

It is essential that leaders are aware of the SEND provision that is offered to those learners with SEN support and with an EHCP. Yet often there can be confusion as to what constitutes SEN provision, what is a reasonable adjustment and what is, in fact, adapted teaching? Are they the same or different?

The argument within the Essential SENCO Toolkit series is that SEN provision, reasonable adjustments and adaptive teaching are different. They each make a specific and valuable contribution, but they are distinct.

Adaptive teaching

Adaptive teaching, inclusive and high-quality teaching are familiar terms to all of us in education. They are referenced by the DfE, Ofsted, Local Authorities, Multi-Academy Trusts, the Education Endowment Foundation and feature within the Teacher Standards and Early Careers Framework. For many of us, adaptive teaching, inclusive teaching, high-quality teaching or other such phrases will feature within our school improvement plans. And such approaches are essential for teaching and learning. Adaptive teaching appeared to 'replace' the term differentiation as colleagues in 'the know' suddenly stopped using the 'd' word and began talking about adaptive teaching. Seemingly replacing one term with another. However, with a closer examination, it does appear that differentiation and adaptive teaching are different concepts. Differentiation can be considered as the altered expectations by teachers, of learner outcomes or performance in lessons. For example, different groups of learners may complete different tasks or different amounts of a task according to expectations. In comparison, the emphasis of adaptive teaching is on teacher responsiveness to learning so the shift is away from what the student has done to a focus on what the teacher is doing. The Education Endowment Foundation in a blog on this subject defined adaptive teaching as **"being responsive to information about learning, then adjusting teaching to better match pupil need"**.

This places the emphasis on the adjustments made by the teacher rather than adjustments made to learner performance, thus making it a far more dynamic and flexible approach. As referenced in Chapter 1, adaptive teaching can be viewed as the personalization of the curriculum offer, relative to learner starting points. The picnic lunchbox analogy presents the curriculum offer as the bread and butter used by the teacher and personalised with relevant and accessible 'fillings' to create a sandwich, which becomes the adapted curriculum offer. In contrast, SEN provision is the yoghurt, i.e. it is additional to or different from the sandwich. A learner with SEN still receives an adapted curriculum offer (their sandwich) but they also receive SEN provision in addition to this (their yoghurt).

Adjustments – reasonable and otherwise

In many ways the term 'adjustment' is both the most simplistic and complicated term of all. It is simple as it refers to tweaks or modifications that are made for a variety of reasons. Within my definition of SEN provision, or action with intent, I describe a balance between adjustments, support/resources and interventions. In this context, I am explicitly referring to teacher tweaks, such as providing verbal instructions instead of written instructions to the learner who has reading as a barrier to learning. Or an adjustment in expectation for the learner who is impulsive and puts his/her hand up at the same time as blurting out their answer. These are simple tweaks that I as the teacher would make. The term 'reasonable adjustment' was introduced with the Equality Act 2010 as a duty placed on settings in relation to disabled children, young people and adults. This duty refers to the requirement to make 'reasonable' changes to enable participation of disabled learners. For example, if a learner has limited mobility and is not able to use the stairs, the law does not expect a school or setting to build a lift, as the costs and time implications for this could be unreasonable. However, it is reasonable for the school or setting to host the lesson in a downstairs room that is accessible for all learners.

Reasonable adjustments are powerful for both the learner, family and school or setting. My perception is that they are an attempt by the law to apply practical problem-solving to meet needs. The duty itself requires a person-centred approach, whereby the disabled learner is central to the identification of the adjustment and the learner, their family and setting together, consider how to reasonably achieve this. Within this process, not only is there the potential to overcome barriers to participation, but the process itself reminds us that at the heart of inclusive practice is our 'shared humanity' (as described by Booth and Ainscow in the Index for Inclusion 2011). After all, as we seek to identify reasonable adjustments, we take time to think about the needs of the learner and their family, but we also consider the needs of the school or setting. The promotion of our 'shared humanity' is also the strength of the shift in our understanding and thinking about neurodiversity as opposed to the pursuit of deficit labelling of differences. We no longer need to define difference as a deficit or as being 'wrong'. Instead, it is simply a different way of being, thinking, communicating or participating. So ultimately, difference is human, which unites all of us.

Adjustments are also at the heart of adaptive teaching. The personalisation of the curriculum, relative to starting points, or indeed to return to our picnic lunch analogy, the choice of sandwich filling based on the needs or preferences of the learner, is part of our everyday practice as educationalists. So, given the overlap between adjustments used in adaptive teaching, the reasonable adjustment duty of the Equality Act 2010 and the adjustments or teacher tweaks which form a part of the SEN provision offer, at times, we may wonder whether these should be the same or different? **The argument here is that the same adjustment could be made as either adaptive teaching, Equality Act compliance and or SEN provision, depending on purpose.** For example, a teacher can provide verbal instructions and check out the learners understanding as part of their approach to adaptive teaching. They can also do this if it is a reasonable adjustment for a disabled learner, and it can be part of the balanced provision offer for a learner with SEN where reading is their identified barrier to learning. Similarly, a learner may be encouraged to change posture shifting from working at a desk to a standing or seated position. This could be an adaptive curriculum adjustment, if the teacher knows that the learner has greater motivation and is more likely to participate with opportunities for movement. It could be a reasonable adjustment if the learner is disabled and has a long term, substantial impairment that needs physical movement to prevent muscle spasms. Or it could be part of SEND provision, if the learner has short attention and or impulsivity as an identified barrier to learning. The important point is that we know *why* we are making the adjustment.

If there is clarity regarding the 'why' of SEND identification and provision, there will be clarity and consistency within implementation. As such, if your quality assurance tasks reveal gaps in what you thought should be happening and what is actually happening, the immediate action is to explore why this is the case. Some Staff may simply not know *how* to deliver expectations or lack confidence in the delivery, experience or training in doing so. For others they may not *know* that was the expectation, or they did know but they didn't agree with the expectation or simply do not share the view that it is their job to do so. And of course, there could be other reasons. Each reason will generate a different response. But to get to this point, you need to know what is happening for your learners with SEND.

Evaluating the implementation of SEND identification and provision is an essential leadership role. Within our settings, we are familiar with deep dives, audits and reviews, some of which are completed internally and some involving external scrutiny. You will undoubtedly, have experienced a range of these over the years, each of which may have generated a varying sense of usefulness. Integrating your own systems for the ongoing self-review of your SEND processes will aid your evaluation of the implementation of SEND in your setting, but needs to become an integral, relevant, but above all, a manageable part of quality assurance. Several years ago, I was asked to work with the Diocese of Norwich Education and Academies Trust (DNEAT), who are a family of 42 academies, to write a bespoke SEND audit tool. But rather than recreating a compliance checklist, which some audit tools can appear to be, we decided to adopt a developmental 'process' rather than a judgemental 'product'. At the heart of the approach was peer review, whereby SENCOs work together to explore and test the evidence of intent, implementation and impact of SEND provision. The annual process begins with each academy collating their own SEND Portfolio of Evidence.

The SEND Portfolio of Evidence

The SEND Portfolio of Evidence is an electronic file, containing 12 folders. The purpose of evidence collation is to enable ongoing reflection and dialogue about the strengths and areas for development in the setting. As indicated below, each of the 12 folders contains a theme which is explored within the self-evaluation form in the SEND Audit Evaluation Prompt. As you read through the list of folders, begin to consider what evidence you would populate in each of these. Some of the examples given, are resources included in Book 1 and Book 2 of the Essential SENCO Toolkit.

Folder 1: Contextual information

Colleagues can include their SEN profile information; SEN, SEND and medical needs profile or Venn diagram; SEN in a nutshell document, or any other preferred 'about us' descriptors.

Folder 2: SEND identification

Information can include the assessment index, teacher concerns or referral forms and the assess, plan, do and review formats.

Folder 3: SEND funding information

This can include a breakdown of the SEN budget received and the annual budget plan along with details of any 'top up' funding or resource spending such as on external agencies and services.

Folder 4: SEND provision and additional adults

In this folder, evidence illustrating TA timetables, bidding records, four functions training or system for deployment, as well as the provision map, personalised provision plans, adjustment, support/resource menus and or an intervention map can be included.

Folder 5: Curriculum and high-quality teaching

This could include information outlining curriculum intent and adjustments for learners with SEND, subject leader statements or any bespoke or individualised curriculum plans for learners with an EHCP.

Folder 6: Impact

Evidence revealing curriculum attainment, personalised attainment and achievements can be included and any other case sampling or studies that demonstrate impact.

Folder 7: Compliance

In this folder evidence would include any review of evaluation of the compliance of the SEN Information Report, accessibility strategy as well as training and qualifications of the SENCO.

Folder 8: Partnership

Include evidence of partnership between staff in school, such as peer coaching or lesson study, as well as partnership with families and external agencies.

Folder 9: Pupil voice

This folder can include information gathered from learner focus groups or interviews, learner questionnaires, extracts from a sample of annual reviews or SEN support reviews that capture learner strengths and areas for development.

Folder 10: Leadership

This could include SEND development plans, defining intent, as well as the professional evaluation collated within the annual strategic planner.

Folder 11: SEND CPD

Including SEND CPD annual plans and impact statements and SENCO and/or SEN Practitioner training themes and priorities.

Folder 12: Other information

This enables personalisation of relevant evidence according to your individual setting and could include attendance information for learners with SEND and or suspension and exclusion data.

The SEND Portfolio of Evidence Audit Evaluation Prompt (AEP)

Contextual Information	SEND Identification	SEND Funding
• What is the SEND Profile? • How many learners on roll? • How is staffing organised? • How much time does the SENCO have and what training do they access? • Is there an SEN governor who meets regularly with the SENCO?	• What systems for identification are used? Assessment tools, teacher referrals, pupil progress meetings? • How is identification of need recorded? • How is the APDR cycle captured? Provision map, learning passports? • Are these systems detailed in the SEN Information Report? • Do all staff and families have a shared understanding of process?	• What is the SEND budget? • How is the budget planned? • How was the budget spent last year and how was it accounted for? • Is top up funding accessed? • What support services are funded?
SEND Provision and Additional Adults (AAs)	**Curriculum and HQ teaching**	**Impact**
• What is the provision offered for learners at SEN Support and with an EHCP? • Is there a balance of adjustments, support/resources, and interventions? • How many AAs are employed, and how are they distributed? • What is the impact of AAs?	• Is the curriculum accessible to all learners? • What adjustments have been made for those with SEND? • Does curriculum intent 'match' curriculum implementation for those with SEND? • What adjustments are made for learners at SEN Support or with an EHCP?	• Are learners with SEND making progress relative to starting points? • Are learners with SEND accessing all opportunities available to their peers? • How confident are staff and families about the lived experiences of learners with SEND at the setting? • Do particular groups of learners have a better or worse experience than others?

Copyright material from Judith Carter (2025), *SEND Leadership*, Routledge

Compliance	Partnership	Pupil voice
- Is the SEN Information Report and SEN policy compliant? - Is the accessibility strategy up to date? - Is there evidence of compliance with the duties within the Equality Act 2010? - Has the SENCO completed the required qualification? - Are parents/carers notified if their child has SEN? How is this evidenced?	- Are families involved in all parts of the APDR cycle? - Do parents/carers understand the SEND system and contribute their expertise? - Are there opportunities for staff to work together to develop practice? - Can the SENCO collaborate with other SENCOs to enhance understanding? - What support services are accessed?	- How involved are learners with their learning? - Are they involved in creating their learning plans and their reviews? - Are they aware of strengths and areas for development? - Do they know what they are working on and why this is useful to them? - Are they encouraged to share their thoughts, reflections, and feelings with staff?
Leadership	**SEND CPD**	**Other information**
- Is the SENCO on SLT or having regular meetings with SLT? - Is SEND a shared leadership priority? - Is monitoring and quality assurance of SEND a shared leadership activity? - Are SEND systems 'led' or simply operationally managed? Is there a shared vision and clarity of purpose? - Are governors active leaders of SEND?	- Are SEND CPD priorities an integral part of the whole school development plan? - Do all staff have opportunities for relevant SEND CPD? - How are activities or topics selected and participation recorded? - What is the impact of SEND CPD?	- Are there differences in attendance between learners with SEND and those without? - Are learners with SEND more or less likely to be suspended or expelled? - Are many learners with SEND also eligible for pupil premium? - What other disadvantaged groups are there in the school? - What are the strengths of SEND provision in the setting and what needs improving?

The advantage of the Portfolio of Evidence is that during the year, SENCOs can collate evidence by dragging and dropping existing files into their portfolio, which acts like a professional electronic 'scrap book' of all things SEND. The rationale for this is to reduce the replication of tasks at times of review. Information is duplicated in so far as it is copied from its original form and placed into the portfolio as evidence samples, but the workload itself does not increase. Often a SENCO or SEN Practitioner may be required to create an 'audit' or Ofsted information file in preparation for an audit or inspection, which in itself becomes a time-consuming process. But by having an ongoing portfolio of evidence, SENCOs are able to access and add information as is appropriate. The SEND Portfolio of Evidence can also be shared with Advisers from the Trust as well as leaders in the academy, local authority or inspectors, and it can be handed over should the SENCO change roles. But most importantly, the portfolio itself becomes part of an ongoing quality assurance and strategic monitoring tool for the SENCO.

The SEND Portfolio of Evidence audit evaluation prompt (AEP) provides an overview of this approach and the SEND Audit evidence ideas (AEI) contains some suggested sources of evidence that could be gathered. The 12 themes help to shape and inform the monitoring and quality assurance activities completed. They help to remind SENCOs and SEN Practitioners of the information that is already in existence, so rather than generating more work, it can help to organise and utilise the work that has already been done.

SEND Audit evidence ideas (AEI)

Contextual Information	SEND Identification	SEND Funding
Venn diagram	Assessment index	Budget planner and costings
SEN profile information	Sample of progress meeting questions/notes Identification flow charts	SEN memorandum or budget statement
SEN in a nutshell	SEN Information Report	Support service 'circle' with costs
Governor meeting agenda Report to governors	Provision map Sample of learning plans or APDRs	
SENCO job description or extract from Code of Practice	Family leaflets outlining the system	
SEND development plan		
SEND Provision and Additional Adults (AAs)	**Curriculum and HQ teaching**	**Impact**
Overview of provision – provision map and/or adjustment menus, support/resources menu, intervention map	Accessibility strategy referencing 'access to the curriculum'	Overview of curriculum attainment, personalised attainment, and achievement of learners with SEND
TA overview – numbers and allocation, job description, time tabling	Adjustment menus and/or core expectation documents for classroom practice	Case sampling summaries
four functions sampling and other impact measures	Curriculum lead statements or overviews	User statements – parent feedback, learner comments
CPD plan for TAs and/or team meeting themes		
SEND QA Toolkit activities		

Compliance	Partnership	Pupil Voice
Completed checklist of SEN Information Report	Sample of APDR meetings showing parental engagement	Sample of learning plans and or one page profiles capturing pupil voice
Copies of SEN Information Report, SEN policy, accessibility strategy	Information for families	Annual Strategic Planner showing planned pupil focus groups or meetings to elicit views
Electronic copy of National Award certificate and or other training	Coaching or professional interest groups	Pupil Questionnaires
Parental notification record or letters	Support service impact statement – annual end of year reflections on each service commissioned	Findings/ Minutes from school council

Leadership	SEND CPD	Other information
Governor reports and SEND updates	SENCO CPD log with reflections	Attendance and exclusion data for learners with SEND
End of year evaluation and action planning	SEND staff training plan and record	SEND and other disadvantaged groups information
Self-evaluation form and or Audit review action plan	Sample of impact statements	
Annual SWOT analysis		

Copyright material from Judith Carter (2025), *SEND Leadership*, Routledge

On the Self Evaluation Summary Sheet, leaders can discuss and consider evidence and then apply a Red/Amber/Green rating to strengths and areas for development. You will notice that in this document there are in fact four categories for consideration: red, red–amber, amber–green and green. The purpose of this was to give additional flexibility regarding the evaluation of development; after all sometimes a more appropriate judgement is 'nearly' amber or 'nearly' green rather than an absolute.

Maria Adcock, Head of School and SENCO within the Kingfisher Federation, is an experienced learning-centred leader for SEND within DNEAT and has completed the peer review audit training. She reports:

> The SEND Portfolio of Evidence is an excellent way to showcase SEND in the school. It captures everything you do as a SENCO in one place! The summary sheet that goes with the evidence is a great tool to use when you need to talk any external agency. When I go and visit a school to complete a SEND peer review it is very helpful to look at the summary sheet before the visit so I can see what the school identifies as strengths and areas for development and whether there are any lines of enquiry I want to explore on the visit. Then, when at the school I can look at the documents in the portfolio to triangulate the evidence. It gives a great overview of SEND in the school.

SEND Portfolio of Evidence – self-evaluation (SE)

Summary sheet

Evaluation Theme	RAAG Rating	Comments
1. Contextual Information		
2. SEND Identification		
3. SEND Funding		
4. SEND Provision and Additional Adults		
5. Curriculum and HQ Teaching		

6. Impact	7. Compliance	8. Partnership	9. Pupil Voice	10. Leadership	11. SEND CPD	12. Other information

The SEND Self-Evaluation took place on:

Those present were:

We identified the following three strengths:

1.

2.

3.

Our three priority areas for development are:

1.

2.

3.

Other comments:

SEND Self-Evaluation – RAAG Rating Prompts

Summary Sheet

Evaluation Theme	Red	Amber/Red	Amber/Green	Green
1. Contextual Information	The contextual information is incomplete, we do not yet have a consistent SEN record and/or our staffing is in flux. Our SENCO time is yet to be protected. There is no named SEN governor.	Our contextual information is complete but fluctuating. There is significant change with numbers on the roll and staffing changes. The SENCO has protected but limited time. There is a named SEN governor but no regular meetings.	We have a clear understanding of our SEND profile and where this fits compared to the national average. Our SENCO time is protected and they work with leadership to review staffing for learners with SEND. The SENCO meets with the SEN governor at times.	Our SEND profile is collated and shared termly and published in our SEN Information Report. The SENCO plans strategic and operational tasks with their time and meets termly with the SEN governor and is on SLT.
2. SEND Identification	We are still determining our SEND identification systems and find it hard to know when a learner has low attainment or SEN. Our paperwork is incomplete.	We know who our learners with SEND are, but our profile information is ad hoc and not easily accessible. Our APDR system is inconsistently applied, and not all learners/families are involved.	We have robust systems for identification and can provide a clear rationale for identification, but our rate is above or below the national average. APDRs are generally completed with learners and their families.	We have a consistent system for identifying learners with SEND, and our staff are confident in applying this. Our profile is within national expectations. Learners and their families are involved in APDRs.

Evaluation Theme	Red	Amber/Red	Amber/Green	Green
3. SEND Funding	We are not yet sure what our SEND funding is or how it is allocated. We have not been able to successfully bid for top-up funding as a result.	We are aware of our SEND funding but cannot yet account for all of the allocation on SEND. This limits our capacity to access top up funding.	We are aware of our SEND funding and can account for the allocation but are not always successful with top-up funding requests. We have not yet been able to show the impact of existing funding.	We can clearly account for our SEND funding and are able to apply for top-up funding successfully when appropriate as we can account for the allocation and impact of funding.
4. SEND Provision and Additional Adults	Our SEND provision is not yet a clear balance of teacher adjustments, support/resources and interventions. It tends to rely on the actions of individuals. TA allocation is fixed and linked to classes.	Our provision aspirations are clearly mapped but not consistently applied. Not all staff are aware of the provision expected for learners with SEND. TA numbers are less than required, so deployment is varied and reactive.	Our provision does match our provision map, but it is not as balanced as it could be. We either rely on interventions or quality teaching adjustments, rather than having a good balance of both. TAs have good relationships with learners and actively support in class.	We have an effective balance of teacher adjustments, support/resources and intervention as our SEND provision and can evidence base anticipated and actual impact. TAs are deployed with purpose and impact.
5. Curriculum and HQ Teaching	Our curriculum is defined, and all teachers are aware of expectations regarding delivery. There is not yet evidence of consistent adaptations, adjustments, or personalisation relevant to the starting point, for learners with SEND.	Our curriculum includes evidence of adjustments and personalisation opportunities for some learners with SEND. The effectiveness of adjustments, adaptations and personalisation is not yet evidence-based via monitoring.	Our curriculum statements include adjustments, adaptations and personalisation for learners with SEND. These are implemented effectively by some members of staff but are not yet consistent throughout the team.	Our curriculum offer is relevant and accessible to all learners, and we know this as we regularly monitor and evaluate it. Staff are trained and consistently confident to adapt and personalise the curriculum to ensure the appropriate sequencing of taught information.

Evaluation Theme	Red	Amber/Red	Amber/Green	Green
6. Impact	Our data shows that learners with SEND are not making progress within the curriculum, and it is hard for us to account for individual progress against targeted outcomes due to inconsistencies with paperwork.	Our experience shows that learners with SEND are making progress with individual targeted outcomes (personalised attainment), but this is hard to 'see' in our records. Curriculum progress for learners with SEND also appears to be static or slow.	Our data shows that learners with SEND are making progress with individual targeted outcomes (personalised attainment), and this is visible in individual records. There is not yet evidence of curriculum progress, and we find it hard to show this.	Our data shows that learners with SEND receive a good 'deal' and are making progress. There is evidence of learning against the curriculum and within individual targeted outcomes (curriculum attainment and personalised attainment.)
7. Compliance	We have published the MAT SEN policy and Information Report.	The SENCO ensures that our policy, SEN Information Report, and Equality Act duties are published on our website, but staff and governors are not yet confident in their understanding or ownership of this.	Our SEN policy, Information Report, and Equality Act 2010 duties are published and understood by staff and governors but we have limited evidence of application or impact.	Our Staff and governors have read Chapter 6 of the Code of Practice and are able to discuss their responsibilities. Our SEN Information Report, access plan, and Equality Act 2010 duties are on our website and understood by all, and our monitoring evidence demonstrates compliance and impact.

Evaluation Theme	Red	Amber/Red	Amber/Green	Green
8. Partnership	Families of learners with SEND may not be aware if they receive core information from staff, and engagement and partnership working is weak. There is limited opportunity for staff collaboration or coaching, or communication with external agencies or governors.	Families of learners with SEND receive core information from staff, but engagement and partnership working is weak. Staff collaboration is good with opportunities for joint planning and coaching.	Families of learners with SEND attend meetings but remain hesitant to engage as partners. There is increasing communication amongst staff and governors and attempts are being made to promote greater consistency of practice.	Communication with learners, families, governors, stakeholders and each other is our top priority. We have highly effective systems for partnership working, and our monitoring systems consistently identify this as a strength.
9. Pupil Voice	APDR cycles are completed by the SENCO or teacher who gives a copy to the learner's family. Learners are not aware of strengths or areas for development.	Learners and families are invited to attend the APDR meetings but are not involved in identifying strengths or areas for development.	Learners attend APDR meetings and, with support, can identify strengths and agree on areas for development. They may not be aware of their targets or actions that will help them.	Learners actively participate in their APDR meetings and identify strengths and areas for development. They are aware of their next steps and can discuss actions that will help them.
10. Leadership	The SENCO is new to the role and will or has just started the statutory qualification. They are not on the leadership team but report to SLT as required. SLT responds to SEND issues as they arise.	The SENCO is qualified and regularly contributes to SLT by providing updates on SEND issues. They provide reports to governors. SLT includes regular opportunities to discuss SEND.	The SENCO is qualified and an active member of SLT. They are relied on by other members of SLT to fulfil all aspects of SEND leadership. They meet regularly with governors. SEND is a priority for SLT, but actions are undertaken by the SENCO.	The SENCO distributes monitoring and QA tasks to other members of SLT and facilitates ownership of SEND by all leaders and governors. There is a shared vision for SEND cultivated by the qualified SENCO.

Evaluation Theme	Red	Amber/Red	Amber/Green	Green
11. SEND CPD	CPD activities are allocated according to individual demand. Development tasks are led by individual practitioners and are not yet part of an overall strategic plan.	The SENCO has created a relevant SEND CPD programme for TAs and those with an interest in SEND. It is not integrated into the whole school development plan.	SEND development activities are integrated into the whole school development plan and have a clearly defined purpose. The impact of activities is not yet recorded and remains anecdotal.	SEND development is an integral part of the whole school improvement plan and CPD programme. There are clear records of CPD activities completed by all staff and the impact of the activities.
12. Other information	Data on our expulsions and suspensions, tribunals and attendance in relation to SEND is not specifically reviewed, and SLT are not yet consistent about identifying vulnerable groups.	Vulnerable groups of learners have been identified, and there is some evidence of over-representation of learners with SEND regarding expulsions and suspensions, but there is not yet an action plan.	Representation of vulnerable groups in attendance, expulsion and suspension data is regularly reviewed by SLT. The SENCO has developed an action plan for addressing concerns.	All information is reviewed considering vulnerable group representation and SLT work with staff, learners and families to address any issues. The promotion of inclusive practice is a whole school value.

These resources are included here as you may wish to adopt or adapt the SEND Portfolio of Evidence as a way of capturing your evidence for the intent, implementation and impact of SEND in your setting. Or this could inspire you to create an alternative structure for evaluation. But establishing a means of collating your evidence is a necessary step to support your evaluation of the implementation of your systems, and the collation of existing information helps to capture what has been achieved but also helps to identify any gaps. Indeed, it was the identification of gaps that SENCOs within the DNEAT MAT discussed as an immediate positive outcome of this process. Simply exploring evidence for each category helped to plan development and next steps. Within DNEAT, academies complete the SEND Portfolio of Evidence and submit the summary evaluation to the Trust on an annual basis. It is then regularly discussed as part of the professional development work with Academies Group Executive Principals. This is also shared and reviewed by SENCO learner-centred leaders during the SEND peer review audit.

SEND review audit tool

A regular system of self or peer review will provide valuable information regarding the implementation of your SEND systems. Completing your own SEND audit review, perhaps with another SENCO or SEN Practitioner from the Trust or a neighbouring school, or as a focused activity of the leadership team, could really help to test out your systems. This can be achieved by sharing information from the Portfolio of Evidence and/or triangulating views by hosting meetings with teachers, TAs, governors, parents/carers and learners themselves. Eliciting views of strengths and areas for development associated with the SEND systems can only help to inform the evaluation of its implementation.

The SEND Portfolio of Evidence is a useful starting point when engaging in a SEND review audit. The self-evaluation form shared earlier in this chapter can form the basis of initial conversations and professional reflections. Triangulating evidence from learning walks, interviews with teachers, TAs, governors, parents/carers and learners themselves can provide invaluable insight into the lived experiences of learners with SEND. To aid your preparation for such an activity, two options for SEND review audits have been identified. The first is the professional dialogue model using the Portfolio of Evidence and the second is a triangulated review audit involving meetings with teachers, TAs, governors, learners and their families. I have provided examples of introductory letters: one with a sample timetable for a professional SEND review audit day, and one with a sample timetable for a triangulated SEND review audit. The inclusion of both is in recognition of your differing starting points and the belief in your right to choose a method that feels most relevant to you at that time. I have been directly involved in both approaches and have experienced merits from each, and, of course, they are not mutually exclusive. Choose a relevant starting point for now and keep the other option available for another time. The list of question prompts contains suggestions that can be adopted or adapted for use during the triangulated SEND review audit.

SEND Review Audit letter with timetable

This timetable can be adopted or adapted as a plan for the SEND review audit day. It assumes that the setting SENCO will be joined by another SENCO or Trust/LA practitioner as well as members of the senior leadership team. This version of the review audit involves professional dialogue and evidence evaluation.

Dear

Thank you for agreeing to work together to review SEND provision. The purpose of this review is to identify strengths and areas for development. During the review we would like to explore all aspects of SEND identification, provision and practice, and will refer to the 12 sections within the SEND Portfolio of Evidence (written by Judith Carter). Our plan for the visit is to spend time in consultation reviewing processes, paperwork and to share a learning walk around the school.

Proposed timings for the visit

9.30 arrival – introductions – consultation focus: sections 1–4 of SEND Self-Evaluation (Context, SEND identification, Funding, Provision and additional adults)

11–12.00 – Learning Walk

12–1.00 – Consultation focus: sections 5–8 (Curriculum and high-quality teaching, Impact, Compliance and Partnership)

1.00–1.30 – Lunch

1.30–3.00 – Consultation focus: sections 9–12 (Pupil Voice, Leadership, SEND CPD, and Other information)

3.00–4.30 – Team completion of self-evaluation and identification of action plan

We look forward to working with you.

Best wishes

Triangulated SEND Review Audit letter with timetable

This timetable can be adopted or adapted as a plan for the triangulated SEND review audit day. It assumes that the setting SENCO will be joined by another SENCO or Trust/LA practitioner as well as members of the senior leadership team. This version of the review audit involves triangulating evidence from meetings with teachers, TAs, learners and families.

Dear

Thank you for agreeing to work together to triangulate and quality assure views on SEND identification and provision. The purpose of this review is to identify strengths and areas for development. During the review we will seek to triangulate views regarding the strengths and areas for development regarding SEND identification and provision in the school. Please adapt the timings according to the school day and invite relevant participants to join us.

Proposed timings for the visit

9.30–11.00 – Time with SENCO to identify the intent of SEND systems and to identify anticipated strengths and areas for development.

11.00–12.00 – Learning Walk
12.00–12.30 – Focus group with teachers
12.30–1.00 – Lunch
1.00–1.30 – Focus group with TAs
1.30–2.00 – Meeting with SEN Governor(s)
2.00–2.30 – Learner Focus Group
2.30–3.00 – Focus group with families
3.00–3.30 – Reflections and recording
3.30–4.30 – Team feedback, SWOT summary and action planning

We look forward to working together.

Best wishes

Recording sheet

Completed by:
Date:
Location:

Summary of discussion:

Strengths:

Areas for development:

Professional evaluation:

Triangulated SEND Review Audit

Question Prompts

Questions for the SENCO

1. Tell me about the SEND profile in your school? (numbers at SEN Support, EHCPs and range of needs?)

2. Do learners with SEND get a 'good deal' in your school?

3. How do you know that?

4. How accessible is the curriculum for learners with SEND?

5. How do curriculum leaders support class and subject teachers to deliver an adapted curriculum relative to learner starting points?

6. Tell me more about SEN provision … how do you ensure a balance between teacher adjustments, support and interventions?

7. How do you ensure that SEN provision is 'additional to or different from' the adapted curriculum offer?

8. How do you know if what a child has learnt in an intervention transfers back into the classroom?

9. How is TA time deployed and what is the impact on learning?

10. How much time do you have for the SENCO role?

11. How is this time utilised? Are you able to carry out strategic as well as operational tasks?

12. Do you meet with the SEN governor and or SLT?

13. How do you support and develop Staff to ensure the best provision for learners with SEND?

14. How is the assess, plan, do and review cycle of SEN Support captured, reviewed and monitored?

15. What do you think are the strengths of SEND provision in the school?

16. What are the priority areas for development?

17. What training have you completed? Did you complete the National Award and or SEND NPQ?

18. How do you maintain your training and professional development? Do you attend any professional networks or groups?

19. Tell me about SEND CPD in the school … do you plan activities and how do you know if they are effective?

20. How confident do you feel about your next Ofsted inspection?

Learning Support Walk – Observation Prompts

Environment
- Does the environment promote independence?
- Is there evidence of a range of learner skills and abilities on display?
- Any evidence of pupil information, provision maps, learning plans?

Resources
- What resources are in the classroom? iPads? Computers? Cameras? Additional adults?
- Are resources being used to support learning?
- Any evidence of support for neurodiversity and or alternative recording?
- Can you see any physical resources that may relate to learners with SEND?

Pupil progress
- Any examples of learning targets, progress or motivational approaches?
- Are learners aware of strengths and targets?
- Any evidence of adapted teaching and or SEND assessment?

Class organisation
- How is the class organised to promote learning for all?
- Is this a fixed layout or do groups change frequently?
- Can you see provision that is 'additional to or different from'?
- Can children explain why they are sitting in particular groups?

Evidence of learning
- Are children/young people learning? Are there groups of learners who are not?
- What impact are the adults having on learning?
- Can learners explain what they are doing?

Engagement
- Are learners engaged in tasks? Is this the same for all learners?
- What is the atmosphere like?
- Are learners encouraged to work things out for themselves or are adults doing it for them?
- Are learners accessing opportunities or is anyone being set up to fail?

Questions for teachers

1. Tell me about SEND in the school and your class(es)

2. How do you adapt the curriculum for all learners?

3. What are some of the barriers to learning experienced by learners with SEND?

4. What adjustments, support or resources and or interventions are made available to learners with SEND in your class(es)?

5. Do you write the SEN support plans?

6. If you have support from TAs, how do you deploy their time? For what purpose?

7. Do you feel supported by the SENCO and other leaders?

8. What SEND themed CPD have you received?

9. Do you feel confident and supported to meet the needs of all learners in your class(es)?

10. Do learners with SEND get a good deal at this school?

11. Do parents/carers share this view?

12. Are your learners with SEND included in friendships?

13. Can you describe three strengths of SEND provision in this school?

14. Can you describe three areas for improvement?

15. Have you read the schools SEN Information Report?

Questions for TAs

1. Tell me about your role.

2. How is your time deployed?

3. Who manages your time and who is your line manager?

4. What training have you received?

5. Do you have opportunities to meet together with other TAs?

6. Is there time to plan and feedback to teachers?

7. What happens if you are off sick? Does anyone cover your work?

8. Do you feel supported by the SENCO and other leaders?

9. Do you feel confident and supported to meet the needs of all learners you work with?

10. Do learners with SEND get a good deal at this school?

11. Do parents/carers share this view?

12. Are learners with SEND included in friendships?

13. Can you describe three strengths of SEND provision in this school?

14. Can you describe three areas for improvement?

15. Have you read the schools SEN Information Report?

Copyright material from Judith Carter (2025), *SEND Leadership*, Routledge

Questions for Governors

1. Tell me about the SEND profile in the school and how this compares to the national?

2. What is the biggest category of need for SEND identification currently (C and L, C and I, SEMH, or P/S)?

3. Do learners with SEND get a good deal at the school?

4. Are they making good progress?

5. How does the school know that?

6. Do you meet with the SENCO regularly?

7. How much time does the SENCO have?

8. Has your SENCO completed the required training?

9. How does your SENCO stay up to date?

10. What CPD is available to staff in school?

11. Are families confident in the provision available to learners with SEND?

12. Are learners with SEND more likely to be expelled from school?

13. Are learners with SEND more likely to have low attendance?

14. Can you describe three strengths of SEND provision in this school?

15. Can you describe three areas for improvement?

Questions for learners

1. Do you like school?

2. What are you good at in school?

3. Is there anything in school that you need help with?

4. Who helps you?

5. What do they do?

6. How does it make a difference?

7. Do you have friends at school?

8. Do you have targets for your learning? What are your targets?

9. Who decided on your targets? Do the targets help you learn more?

10. Are you asked to share your thoughts and ideas about learning and whether you want help?

11. How do you know you are learning?

12. Can you talk to teachers about learning or any worries you have?

13. Would you recommend this school to other learners?

14. Tell me three good things about being at this school?

15. Tell me three things the school could do to be even better?

Questions for families

1. Do you think children with SEN-D are supported at this school?

2. How does the school identify children with SEN?

3. Who is the SENCO and what is their role?

4. How do you know if your child is making progress?

5. What information do you receive from the school about your child's learning?

6. Do you get an opportunity to contribute to the planning and review of their learning?

7. What support does your child get? Has this made a difference?

8. How involved in their own learning are your children?

9. What would you do if you thought your child was not making progress?

10. Do you know how to complain about the treatment or support on offer?

11. Are children with SEND bullied in school?

12. Do you look at the school website? Have you seen the SEN Information Report?

13. Do you have confidence in the school?

14. Can you describe three strengths of SEND provision in this school?

15. Can you describe three areas for improvement?

Team meeting discussion prompt

1. How are we feeling?

2. What have we noticed about the day?

3. Were there any surprises?

4. What are the strengths?

5. What are the areas for development?

6. What has been recorded within our SWOT forms?

7. Are you particularly pleased about anything from the day?

8. Are you disappointed about anything from the day?

9. Do you have enough information to write an action plan?

10. Has this been a useful process?

Sarah Smith is the SENCO and Deputy Head at Kessingland Primary Academy and is also a learning centred leader for SEND within DNEAT. Sarah regularly leads triangulated SEND review audits using this approach and reports:

> The SEND Portfolio of Evidence provides a structure to help schools self-reflect and evaluate how they support learners with SEN. When completing our collaborative peer reviews the portfolio helps us identify areas to explore further and evidence the school may have in place. With the SEND Portfolio of Evidence, teachers have felt confident and prepared for supportive and challenging conversations and have been able to reflect ahead of the visit to make the most out of the day. The SEND Portfolio of Evidence helps guide our conversations and provides a broad overview of what it is like to be a learner with SEND in their school. It allows us to understand the context and profile of the school as well as learn more about the provision in place. The portfolio guides an open and honest conversation and supports schools to reflect on their own actions moving forward.

Action planning

An essential element of any SEND audit or review is the generation of an action plan. Within the developmental model adopted by DNEAT academies, it was agreed that the host academy, would write their own action plan using information generated and exchanged during the SEND peer review audit day, rather than receiving a report written by the reviewers. The rationale for this is a belief that change is most effective when it is 'owned' and 'driven' by those who will be most affected by the change. It is the school leaders and their community that will bring about meaningful change in any setting, and this will be far more effective than external attempts at change. Within this model, action planning becomes part of a shared conversation and evidence exchange during the day but specifically at the team meeting at the end of the day. Emerging themes are shared as strengths, weaknesses, opportunities and threats (SWOT) and information gathered is left with the academy to help inform their own priorities. I have provided an action plan format that you might wish to adapt or adopt, followed by a SWOT analysis sheet for use during the review process. If the prospect of engaging in a formal peer review feels too daunting at this time, simply asking senior leaders and or staff to complete a collaborative SWOT analysis could be incredibly revealing and useful for your immediate SEND development planning.

SEND Review Audit

Academy Action Plan

Date of visit:
Review team:
Action plan written by:
Date of action plan
To be reviewed by:

Key points discussed:

Our identified strengths:

Our identified areas for development:

Immediate actions we will be taking and by when:

Longer term actions we will be taking, by when:

Additional support:

Our reflections about the process:

Our rating scale feedback of the process, where 10 is the highest mark and 1 is the lowest:

1   2   3   4   5   6   7   8   9   10

Inferred Strengths, Weaknesses, Opportunities and Threats

Weaknesses	Threats
Strengths	Opportunities

Implementation

Reflections

- How do you know what is happening for learners with SEND?
- How often are learning support walks carried out?
- Do you meet with families, learners, teachers and TAs to elicit their experiences and views?
- Have you ever used your SEN Information Report to 'test out' the implementation of SEN systems?

Actions to consider

- Create 12 electronic folders and begin to drag and drop existing evidence into this one Portfolio of Evidence. Notice what evidence you have and any themes that are limited or missing.
- Identify a SENCO 'buddy' who may also be interested in participating in a shared SEND review audit. Talk together about this and, if in agreement, take it to the heads of each setting, outlining the intent, implementation requirements and anticipated impact.
- If a full peer SEND review audit is not yet realistic in your role, identify opportunities to triangulate information gathering from learners, families and staff. Can this form part of your QA annual strategic plan?

6. Impact

The Collins Dictionary defines impact as "to impact on a situation, process, or person means to affect them". And as a countable noun they say, "the impact that something has on a situation, process, or person is a sudden and powerful effect that it has on them". In education, so many of our actions are determined by the anticipated effect that they will have on learners. The irony is that *everything* that we choose to do, or indeed not do, has an impact; the question is whether this impact is positive or negative? Think about the SEND system and the very process of identifying a learner as requiring SEN Support. This decision triggers the requirement for provision that is 'additional to or different from' that ordinarily available to others of the same age. And the quality and diversity of that provision in terms of the relevance to the individual learners' strengths and barriers to learning, will predetermine the effect it may have on them.

The purpose of the 7 Cs Learning Portfolio is to give teachers a language of strengths and barriers to learning, to empower them to identify more accurately actions that could potentially overcome or if possible, to remove barriers, rather than simply offering more of the same. As is stated in various places in the Essential SENCO Toolkit, if a learner is falling behind in maths, of course they continue to receive adapted maths relative to their starting point, as this is their curriculum offer, but if they are identified as having SEN then they should receive provision that is 'additional to or different from' this too. When evaluating the impact of our SEND systems, we should be evaluating the impact of the provision that is additional to or different from, and considering the difference this has on learner access and progress with these skills, and in turn, their access and progress with the curriculum. But what difference do we anticipate would have occurred?

Triangulated impact

Capturing impact is far more effective when we have clearly defined our anticipated impact, or our intent. Similarly, when we have actively monitored, reviewed and quality assured the implementation of our provision. With both of these in place, impact is far more visible and measurable. So often in education our language of progress, refers to curriculum attainment. This is of course our 'bread and butter' and a key priority for all learners, including those with SEND. Yet attending to this alone, undermines the rationale of the 'additional to or different from' element of SEN Support, or indeed the very purpose of the production of an Education, Health and Care Plan. In addition to curriculum attainment, these actions with intent (SEN provision) could be evaluated as personalised attainment, where consideration can be given to the impact of targeted outcomes. Similarly, consideration should also be given to achievement, as achievement and personalised attainment will undoubtedly influence curriculum attainment.

Curriculum attainment – information acquired and demonstrated by the learner against the taught criterion of curriculum subjects.

Personalised attainment – information acquired and demonstrated by the learner in relation to their individualised learning plans. This could be as part of the 'assess, plan, do, review' cycle and include progress with targeted outcomes described on learning plans or progress summarised for annual reviews.

Achievement – personal goals or accomplishments. This could include learning to ride a bike, travel on a bus, the completion of a computer game level, being able to stay in the classroom or arrive confidently at school if this had previously been a barrier. Achievements are as individual as all of us and should be captured and valued as they are interconnected to curriculum and personalised attainment.

Accounting for curriculum attainment, personalised attainment and achievement of learners with SEND, strengthens the evidence base of their 'lived experience' at school. It can also tell the 'story' behind the curriculum data and help to demonstrate why progress is still visible and impactful, even if curriculum attainment is below expected. Of course, it does not mean our ambition for curriculum attainment declines, on the contrary, it can be evidence of greater ambition as we are attempting to overcome or if possible, remove barriers that are impeding access to the curriculum. Equally our ambition for impact is not restricted to one of the triangulated measures, but rather we remain committed to progress in all areas of curriculum attainment, personalised attainment and achievement. Triangulating progress measures in this way reinforces the strengths-based approach of learners as a 'whole' child or young person, not just a vessel to receive curriculum information. It enables personalisation and individuation whilst

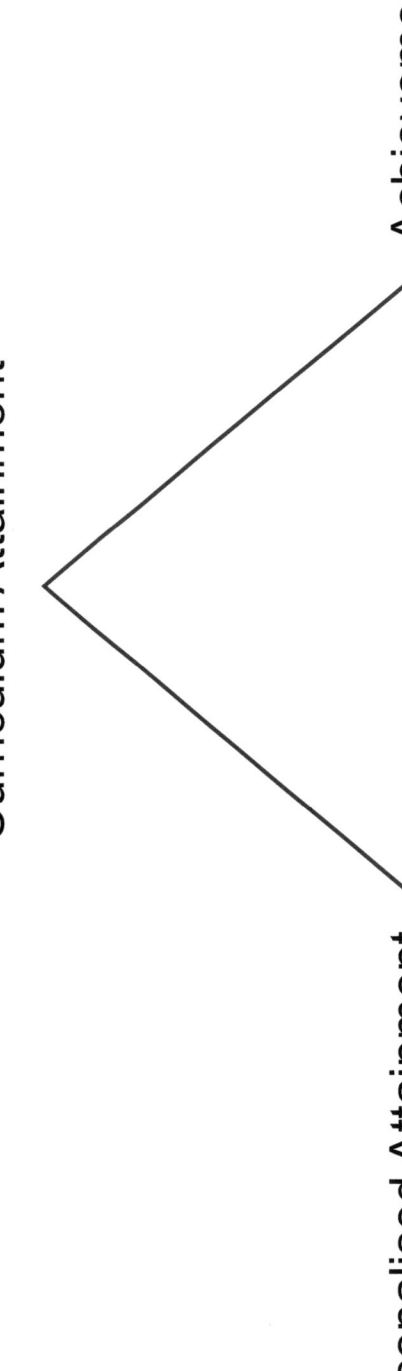

also providing a thorough overview of all aspects of their learning and engagement in a period of time.

Louise McGregor SENDCO at Thurston CE Primary Academy shared a drawing that she created as a visual prompt to illustrate how the 7 Cs Learning Portfolio impacts the whole child. She describes this a useful reminder of the elements of the 7 Cs.

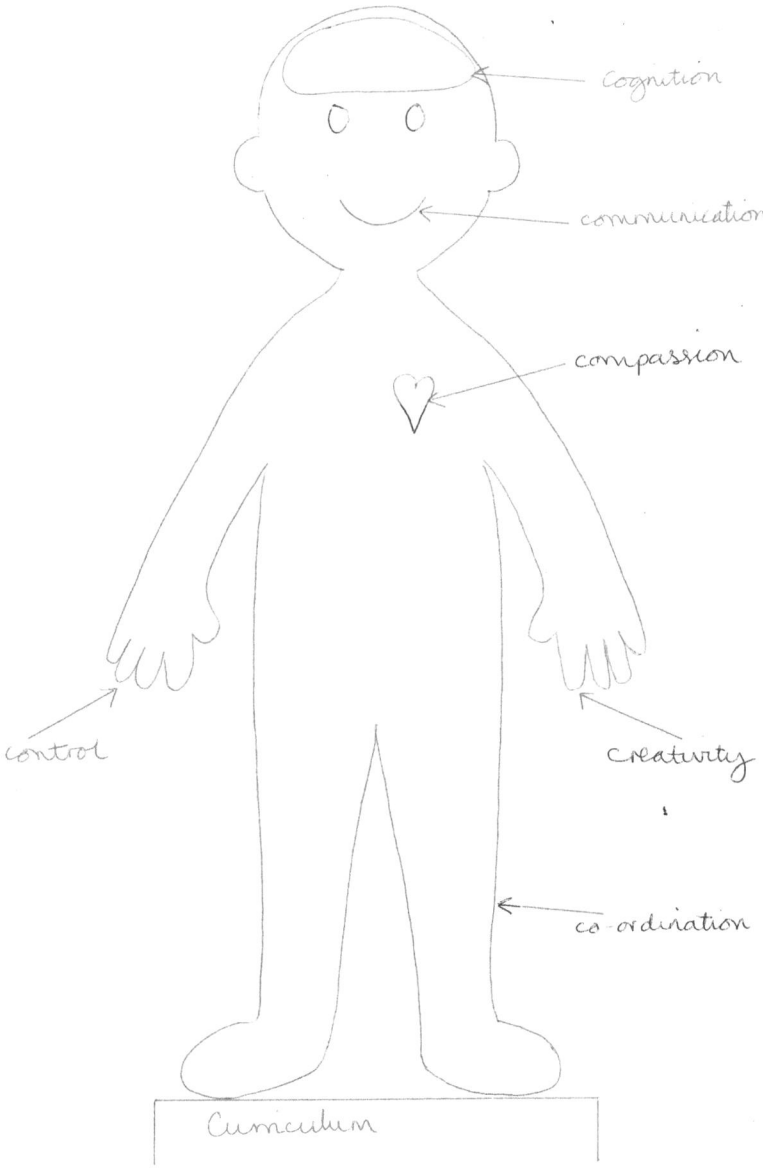

Impact and targeted outcomes

As leaders of SEND, anticipated and actual impact are vitally important to our evaluation of the effectiveness of the system. These can be evidence-based from scrutiny of various sources including, learner engagement, parental confidence, staff knowledge and, of course, through the individualised graduated approach or APDR cycles. But for the latter to have relevance, our staff, working with learners and their families, need to create relevant targeted outcomes as these capture the planned intent, implementation and anticipated impact of SEN support. Without relevant targeted outcomes, the nature of the SEN support may lack clarity, consistency and ultimately accountability.

Targeted outcomes are a way of combining a learning goal with the anticipated impact of that goal. For example, a target could be 'to learn to write 5 more words'. It becomes a SMART target (specific, measurable, achievable, relevant and time related) if it provides additional detail. However, an outcome refers to the 'difference' that this skill would have on the learner. The outcome of the above example could be, 'to be able to write a birthday card for Mum'. Combining the two approaches into a targeted outcome can help to connect purpose and application. For example: "Judith will learn to write 5 more words, SO SHE CAN write a birthday card for her Mum". This scaffold can be useful to aid teacher connection between the target and the anticipated impact of the target. However, it can still create a disconnect, unless the targeted outcome directly links to the area for development and relates to the anticipated change, relative to starting point. This can be captured using the ABC-D scaffold for targeted outcomes.

The ABC-D scaffold for targeted outcomes

A – Area for development/Attribute

B – Baseline

C – Change

D – Do

ABC-D scaffold for targeted outcomes

A	Area for development/ Attribute	Description of barriers or learning attributes to be developed
B	Baseline	Describe the starting point in real terms
C	Change	Define the change that is anticipated
D	Do	List the actions to be undertaken and the impact – I want you to do this SO YOU CAN do that

This ABC-D scaffold can support teachers when writing targeted outcomes, whether using the 7 Cs Learning Portfolio or not. Any target can be enhanced by ensuring the connections between the area for development or learning attribute, current baseline or starting point, the anticipated change and with reference to the actions to be undertaken. The examples presented here do relate to the 7 Cs Learning Portfolio but any area for development can be identified.

Example 1

Area for development/Attribute: Control – Self-regulation – **Impulsivity**.

Baseline: Judith called out 18 times in a ten-minute observation during a whole-class teaching session.

Change: Judith will call out nine times in a ten-minute observation during a whole-class teaching session (50% reduction).

Do: Judith will take part in twice weekly games involving a 'hold' or 'freeze' element, SO SHE CAN rehearse the skill of holding an impulse and apply these skills to other contexts.

In school: Games with Mr(s) Jones Tuesday and Thursday lunchtimes.

At home: Family game of musical statues when visiting grandparents.

When out and about: Judith will play 'sleeping lions' and 'what's the time Mr Wolf' when playing out with friends or siblings.

Example 2

Area for development/Attribute: Cognition – **Working memory.**

Baseline: James can remember and follow one instruction at a time.

Change: James will remember and follow two-part instructions.

Do: James will take part in a working memory group twice weekly with four other children rehearsing skills of digit and object recall, forwards and backwards and playing memory games, SO HE CAN refine the skill of holding information and apply this to retaining instructions given by his teacher.

In school: Working Memory group on Monday and Wednesday afternoons (20 minutes).

At home: James will collect one or two items from different rooms in the house on request.

When out and about: When shopping with Dad, James will collect two items as requested.

Example 3

Area for development/Attribute: Communication – **Expressive vocabulary.**

Baseline: Clare has a small pool of words to use in speech and finds it hard to name objects and feelings.

Change: Clare will have a range of emotion words and be able to use these in speech when describing her feelings.

Do: Clare will work with Mr(s) Jones and three other children to identify words and pictures that describe feelings and link these to their own prior experiences SO SHE CAN use words to describe her feelings when asked in the day.

In school: 20 minutes group time weekly for three weeks.

At home: Talking about the feelings of characters in story books.

When out and about: Asking and answering questions with family members about feelings.

Sharing the ABC-D scaffold with teachers could facilitate a useful dialogue regarding the writing of relevant and purposeful targeted outcomes. A natural extension of this will be the consideration of 'whom' the targeted outcomes are actually written for? Ultimately, targeted outcomes should be written with learners themselves and should have meaning and relevance to them. If we shift to a child centred approach to targeted outcomes, the wording can be modified as illustrated in the same examples below:

Example 1

Area for development/Attribute: Control – Self-regulation – **Impulsivity** – I have lots of ideas that burst out of me!

Baseline: The teacher counted that I called out 18 times in ten minutes during English.

Change: I'm going to try to hold some of my thoughts so when the teacher counts next time, I will only call out nine times in ten minutes.

Do: I'm going to play musical statues and 'hold it' games with Mrs Jones and three other children twice a week at lunchtime SO I CAN practice holding my words and actions.

Example 2

Area for development: Cognition – **Working Memory** – I listen but I can't always remember what has been said.

Baseline: I can remember one thing at a time.

Change: I want to be able to remember two things that are said to me.

Do: I will work with Mr Jones and four friends to play memory games SO I CAN see if this helps me to remember two things in the classroom.

Example 3

Area for development: Communication – **Expressive Vocabulary** – I find it hard to think of some words especially about my feelings.

Baseline: I stay quiet when I am asked how I feel or shrug my shoulders.

Change: I want to be able to use words to describe when I feel happy, sad, worried, excited and unsure.

Do: I will work with Mrs Jones and three friends to look at pictures and words that describe feelings SO I CAN use these words or pictures when I am asked how I feel.

What did you notice as you read these examples? Which version offered the greatest clarity? Adopting a child-centred approach to targeted outcomes can boost relevance and accessibility of target setting and support both the learner, their family and the teacher to really understand what they are working on, why they are working on this instead of something else and how they will know it makes a difference.

Kathy Spurgeon, acting assistant headteacher and SENCO at the Federation of Fairfield Infant and Colneis Junior School, reports:

> We now hold specific SEN pupil parent meetings each term where targets from the 7 Cs are discussed with all involved. This helps the teacher, pupil and parent to understand their role and responsibilities. The SEN termly targets now amalgamate the one page profiles and we use the targets as our assess, plan, do, review approach. The next stage is to bring in the 4 functions of learning support – to disseminate with all staff and to begin to build this into the learning framework within school.

The language of the 7 Cs Learning Portfolio combined with the ABC-D scaffold for targeted outcomes can support staff to write relevant and meaningful targets with learners and their families. Emma Beck, SENCO at Wells Primary Academy and Burnham Market Primary Academy, reports:

> The 7 Cs approach has transformed our way of thinking around what support our pupils need. Our SEND support plans now outline strengths, areas for development and targeted outcomes using the language of the 7 Cs and our support plans are better than ever!

Similarly, Jacqui Harris, SENDCO at Firside Junior school and Kinsale Junior School, reports

> We love the way the pupil voice is the focus and it works on the children's strengths. Having opportunities to involve families with the children's targets and incorporating what they can do at home has also helped to build on those

home/school relationships and ultimately support the children with making progress. It is a working document with a purpose!

Case sampling

Case sampling can also be a useful tool for SEND leaders to help monitor and quality assure the impact of the system. As the name suggests, monitoring and quality assurance activities can focus on a sample of individual learners and explore their lived experience and associated impact of SEND provision. By evaluating the paper-trail, observing and interviewing the learner, their family and staff, a picture will emerge about what is working well and what needs further development. Case sampling is different to a case study as sampling involves triangulation, testing and evaluation, whereas a case study can often be presented as a narrative or an account. Once again, the role of professional evaluation is the key. To aid this process of evaluation, a case sampling QA recording sheet is included. It is intended to be a working document, that you complete whilst undertaking specific tasks which you can then analyse and evaluate. As always, please adapt or adopt the document, and do keep in mind that this is not an activity that is undertaken for all learners with SEND. The time implication of that would be incredible, so please do not even consider that. But, when possible, choose a learner and attempt to gather the information as part of your 'testing' of the lived experience of the learner.

Quality assurance activity: case sampling

Completed by:	Date:

Learner profile
Name:	Date of birth:
Age:	Year group:
SEN support/EHCP:	Category of need:

Date of recent APDR:
Strengths identified:

Areas for development/Attributes identified:

Provision expected:
Types of adjustments:

Support/resources:

Interventions:

Additional information
Curriculum attainment:

Personalised attainment:

Achievement:

Attendance:
Exclusions:
Clubs:

Learning walk:

What I anticipate:

Actual experience:

Evaluation:

Teacher consultation and book look:

Evaluation:

Learner consultation:

Evaluation:

Parent/carer consultation:

Evaluation:

SENCO analysis:

What is working well:

What needs further development:

Actions:

Implications for SEND systems and or training

Case sampling can also be an ongoing 'thread' of quality assurance and monitoring. Rather like a case study, actions undertaken and the impact of these on learner outcomes, triangulated attainment and their lived experience in the setting can be reviewed. Although this can sound daunting and time consuming, you and the learner's teacher are probably already doing this but not necessarily recording it. You will be very aware of individual learners and their experiences in school, but this may not be formally captured. Protecting time to capture this information and to formally evaluate impact using case sampling, will provide invaluable evidence of the effectiveness of your SEND systems. And of course, do remember, this is a litmus test, i.e. a small sample, it is not a task to be completed for every learner on your SEND record.

Learner perspective form

As leaders of SEND, it is essential that we evaluate our systems from the perspective of learners themselves. What is it like to be a learner in this setting? Do I feel safe? Do I have friends? Do I feel valued and empowered to share my thoughts, observations and questions? Do I understand the language and the environment around me? Can I access the language and environment around me. Am I represented in the learning community? Are my family represented? Am I happy and curious? The learner perspective form can aid leader evaluation of the learner's lived experience of the SEND systems. This approach encourages an exploration of experiences and the collation of evidence to answer the ten questions. This can be an essential tool for SEND leadership and is invaluable during the SEND audit/review process as it is a powerful reminder of the intent of an SEND system. **Reflecting on the experiences of learners is the ultimate measure of impact.** Evaluating these questions may generate additional information gathering such as learner focus groups or simple questionnaires which can be distributed by members of the school council, learning mentors and or teachers which can help to shape next steps.

Learner perspective form

Use this form to reflect on what it may be like to be a learner with SEND in your setting. Consider whether …

If I am a learner with SEND in this setting:

1. Do I understand what is going on around me? (Can I access the environment, follow information and routines?)

2. Do I feel safe and happy?

3. Do I have friends and if not? Is there anything that might help me to make friends?

4. Am I learning and are the people around me ambitious for me to learn?

5. Do I know I am learning, and can I apply my learning?

6. Are my parents happy and confident with the support offered?

7. Can I take part in other opportunities like clubs and trips, just like other children?

8. Is my work and voice valued?

9. Am I given 'help' (adjustments, support/resources and interventions) that are relevant to my needs?

10. Is the curriculum really accessible to me?

Reflections

- How do you capture impact?
- Where is the evidence of this and who do you 'report' this to?
- Could a triangulated measure of impact reveal the 'story' behind curriculum attainment?
- Would the ABC-D scaffold for writing targeted outcomes support your staff?
- How accessible and relevant are your existing targets to learners themselves?
- Would case sampling help to quality assure impact for an individual learner?

Actions to consider

- Share the ABC-D scaffold for writing targeted outcomes with staff and promote the connection between impact and accurate baselining of targets.
- Take a closer look at the case sampling form and identify a few sections to start with. Remember to adapt as feels most relevant.
- Share the learner perspective form within a senior leadership meeting and identify where the evidence for this is?

7. Practical Management

As the title suggests, within this chapter we are going to explore some of the practical management approaches of SEND leadership using the Essential SENCO Toolkit. I suspect that if I were reading this book rather than writing it, this would be the chapter I would turn to first! Time is so limited for all of us, and the practical application of ideas is essential. Throughout the trilogy of books, we have shared and evolved key themes that relate to SEND assessment, intervention and leadership and this chapter is intended to interleave ideas with practical management. So, let's get started and explore the practical management of SEND leadership using the Essential SENCO Toolkit. The ten themes for consideration are:

1. Introducing the language of the 7 Cs Learning Portfolio to staff, learners and families
2. Identifying a starting point for the use of the four functions of learning support
3. Supporting staff confidence and competence with writing relevant targeted outcomes
4. Promoting learner participation within the assess, plan, do and review cycle using the 7 Cs
5. Using the 7 Cs Progress Tracker
6. Quality assurance as a leadership tool
7. The adoption of a strengths-based approach
8. Setting up a SEND Portfolio of Evidence
9. Evaluating the SEND system from a learner's perspective
10. The implementation of EHCPs

DOI: 10.4324/9781003408994-8

1. Introducing the language of the 7 Cs Learning Portfolio to staff, learners and families

The first step in this process is ensuring your own knowledge and confidence with the key principles of the 7 Cs. This includes a shared belief in a strengths-based approach, an understanding of the 49 learning attributes contained within the 7 Cs Learning Portfolio and clarity of expectations regarding the implementation of the assess, plan, do and review cycle at SEN support. From this position, you can host a staff meeting and introduce the 7 Cs, including the origami task booklet, and encourage all teachers to identify three strengths and three areas for development within their next SEN Support meeting. I have had the privilege of working with staff on the introduction of this approach and never tire of the positive reaction to the language of the 7 Cs. The majority of colleagues report to value the simplicity of the approach and the language 'feels' relevant and accessible. Obviously being strengths-based is more than just the identification of three strengths to bring balance to the three areas for development, but it is a practical starting point for teachers. This 'quick win' will promote engagement with the learner and their family and help to promote connection and collaboration.

As your teachers become more confident with this approach to SEN support meetings and identifying strengths and areas for development, you can begin to roll out the language of the 7 Cs to families and learners themselves. The family leaflets contained in Book 2: *SEND Intervention: Planning Provision with Purpose* can be a useful introduction and can be shared with families or included in your SEN Information Report or website. And of course, don't ever underestimate the power of conversation! Consider hosting a family forum or SEND coffee morning or afternoon where you can share the approach and once again complete the origami booklet task, this time with families. Reinforce with families the importance of identifying strengths and promoting a language of challenge rather than difficulty, development rather than improvement and, importantly, of asking learners themselves to identify what they think their strengths are. Learners will have a very clear sense of what they find challenging but may not always be aware of their strengths. Encouraging them to talk about activities they enjoy and showing curiosity can in itself help learners to begin to 'notice' more about themselves. Of course, it is unrealistic to wait for learners or their families to use the same language of the 49 attributes within the 7 Cs Learning Portfolio and this is not necessary. Instead, listen to the learner or family member and then map their descriptions onto the learning profile. For example, if a child describes themselves as a junk modeller or reports loving building with Lego, encourage them to tell you about their latest model or project and share with them that in "my little book, this comes under creativity and making things. Shall we identify making things as one of your strengths?" Similarly, talk about areas that feel more tricky for them and map these against the 7 Cs as areas for development.

Allison McLellan, Vice Principal and SENCO at Hellesdon High School, has found that:

> The 7 Cs approach gives us the ability to follow a more strengths-based approach to support and assessment. Through a shared language it is easier to identify challenges that pupils have and offer a tailored approach to support this. With parents, children and school staff embracing these principles, we have been able to foster an inclusive environment that celebrates strengths and specifically targets areas for development in a meaningful and impactful way.

The strength of the 7 Cs is that it is a language, and as such it is adaptive and flexible and can promote conversation. In a world where much of our interactions are automated and electronic, it is so refreshing to value and protect time for conversation. SEN support meetings should ultimately be considered as a purposeful conversation between teachers, learners and their families. Of course, there has to be 'evidence' of the assess, plan, do and review conversation, but the 'paperwork' really should be secondary to the conversation. As it is the conversation that will bring about change and the paperwork should simply be a record of that. When time allows, try to find your own starting point for rolling out the language of the 7 Cs, whether that is to all staff, or to particular year groups or classes to begin with. Certainly, the comments below from practitioners who have done this, would suggest that it is worth a try.

Donna Garratt, SENDCO at Acle St Edmund Primary Academy, reports:

> The 7 Cs has been a really supportive tool for the staff to use in school. It has supported staff to look beyond curricular outcomes and has enabled the children to make measured progress and to celebrate their successes. We are looking forward to enhancing its use in supporting our children and involving our families more.

Jennie Gregson, SENDCO at Arden Grove Infant and Nursery School, has found:

> Using the 7 Cs approach and suggested structures around it has helped us to see the process of developing support plans with fresh eyes and increase their value even further. Although we have always highlighted children's strengths within this process, with Judith's support we have re-framed how we use this information and the 'lightbulb' moments we have had when we feel we have collectively and successfully woven a child's strengths into how we support them to overcome a barrier to learning have been a real joy.

2. Identifying a starting point for the use of the 4 Functions of Learning Support

The starting point for using the 4 Functions of Learning Support as a method for capturing the deployment of TA time is your confidence and knowledge of the 4 Functions of Learning Support. When time allows, re-read the chapters within Book 2: *SEND Intervention: Planning Provision with Purpose* and evaluate your clarity and confidence about purposeful TA deployment as either mediation, reinforcement of a skill or learning behaviour, assessment or intervention. From here, you may choose to host an initial meeting or training session with TAs to introduce the 4 Functions and promote a discussion around the activities that they complete and which ones they would define as mediation, reinforcement, assessment or intervention. Together, you may then choose a particular function to focus on in more detail. For example, exploring Feurstein's concept of a mediated learning experience (MLE) and the essential requirement of intentionality, reciprocity, meaning and transcendence and how to create that within interactions with individuals or small groups. Similarly, working together to identify useful mediation questions and then having a go at using the questions in interactions. Exploring the potential and application of the TA 'assessment' function is also a useful starting point and one that I think is underused in settings generally. As we know, many outside agencies will ask to complete an observation of a learner (myself included as part of my 'day' job as an Educational Psychologist). Yet as soon as we enter the classroom we change the dynamic. For some learners their behaviour becomes more regulated and controlled (even though that may not be the case at other times); others may become anxious and either retreat or become distracted, impulsive or seek to gain the attention of the new 'audience'. Either way, the 'snapshot' is not as 'typical' as may be hoped. Yet our TAs are part of the class and therefore their presence is 'typical'. This makes them well-placed to gather information for teachers and or SENCOs. Training TAs to complete tally observations, checklist observations and verbatim observations can be exceptionally useful at gathering information for the teacher or SENCO to analyse, and this could be your starting point.

The Education Endowment Foundation remind us that an essential requirement of TA deployment is training and preparedness. The 4 Functions of Learning Support can help to structure your training for TAs, and taking the assessment function as an example, can be used to teach specific skills. For example, a tally observation involves recording the frequency of a particular behaviour, action or word within a timed interval. For a learner with impulsivity as an area for development, this can be incredibly useful to inform a baseline of impulsive actions or comments. TAs can be trained to record the frequency of calling out or an impulsive action during a ten-minute interval. This can of course be repeated over time to help capture evidence of changes. A checklist observation can also be useful for TAs as the teacher and the SENCO can create a checklist of actions, behaviours or words that the TA will look out for and check off when they are seen within a specific timed interval. A checklist can include positive actions, behaviours or words as well as those that are seeking modification. The checklist should be personalised for the individual learner and identified by the commissioner of the information gathering, i.e. the teacher and or SENCO. Finally, training TAs to complete verbatim observations can be incredibly useful, as this information can support professional conversations and aid future planning. It is essential that TAs are trained to deliver these approaches so they feel confident to gather the information as requested.

The identification of your starting point really is your choice and there are no right or wrongs. Stay focused on purpose or as we discussed a few chapters ago, the intent for this action and your anticipated impact of this action, and then have a go. At a time, where budgets are increasingly restricted, utilising the framework of the 4 Functions of Learning Support could help to structure development and training opportunities for TAs at very little additional cost, other than time.

Sally-Ann Hewitt-Coleman, SENCO at Open Academy, worked with colleagues to implement the 4 Functions of Learning Support across their secondary setting. She reports:

> We have been using 7 Cs and the 4 Functions as 'MARI a TA' approach. This has worked well as teachers have been very used to the acronyms of mediation, assessment, reinforcement and intervention (MARI), although the order has changed, it remains in teachers' minds. The section on professional prompt sheets has been used by teachers in CPD and we used the 7 Cs language to add to our provision maps and support plans. The 7 Cs were invaluable.

3. Supporting staff confidence and competence with writing relevant targeted outcomes

The ABC-D framework shared in Chapter 6 is intended to support the practical management of staff confidence and competence with writing relevant targeted outcomes. Explicitly teaching staff to identify areas for development, to define a baseline in real terms and to describe the change they want to see, will help to scaffold their writing of relevant targeted outcomes. **Too many SEN support targets relate to the curriculum offer rather than the 'additional to or different from'**, the classic example being a reading or spelling target for a learner with impulsivity as an area for development. Of course, the reading or spelling target is relevant but as part of their adapted curriculum offer if the reason for SEN identification is impulsivity or self-regulation. The targeted outcome in this example, should focus on the rehearsal of control and or positive steps to regain regulation and self calm.

A useful method to support staff is to share the writing of targeted outcomes within a staff meeting. This opportunity promotes collaboration and pooling of ideas and lends itself to the modelling of positive examples. Structuring thinking using the ABC-D framework should promote connections between the area for development/attribtues, the existing baseline information and the anticipated change, which will ultimately set teachers up positively to evaluate impact. Staff collaboration on the wording of targeted outcomes protects thinking time and promotes development opportunities and peer support and challenge.

Amy Healy, SENCO at Debenham High School, reports:

> I work in a mainstream secondary school and I have used the 7 Cs to identify and set targets for IEPs. I feel like the 7 Cs model gave teachers knowledge and

language to identify what the students were really struggling with. This has been very well received by staff and I think the areas identified as barriers to learning and next steps are really having an impact on supporting students in school.

The ABC-D scaffold for targeted outcomes is a tool for SEND leadership as greater relevance and accuracy within target setting, particularly clarity over starting points, will aid the demonstration of impact.

4. Promoting learner participation within the assess, plan, do and review cycle using the 7 Cs

As obvious as it sounds, the first and arguably the most important way of promoting learner participation within the assess, plan, do and review cycle, is to ensure attendance and engagement at the SEN support meetings, or indeed the annual review for learners with an EHCP. This is both in terms of the learner physically meeting with the teacher and their family on a termly or half termly basis, but also ensuring that learners understand the purpose of SEN support or their EHCP. It is incredibly important that SEN identification and support is not seen as a negative or a sign of weakness or failure, but rather a method for collaboratively looking for strengths and sharing ideas to support areas for development. All of us have areas for development and promoting a culture that values our individual learning profiles is part of effective SEND leadership.

The language of the 7 Cs Learning Portfolio can really aid shared understanding of learning attributes, and the user guide within Book 1 is written to be shared with learners and families. Staff can begin by clarifying the purpose of the meeting, the time available and asking the learner and family members to identify strengths. The teacher can also share their observations of the learners' strengths. If there are different views, these should all be valued and can either be recorded as a commentary or a consensus may be made. The essential element is that all views are valued and heard. Similarly, when identifying areas for development, ask the learner to identify what they find tricky and what they have noticed that helps them with this. Begin a conversation about barriers to learning or areas for development using the language of the 7 Cs to aid reflection and consideration. Once again, ideally a consensus will be reached which identifies three areas for development which will be used to inform the ABC-D of the targeted outcomes. However, if the learner has a different priority for development, this should be included into their plan. It may be useful to reassure teachers that there is nothing 'magical' about the identification of 'three' strengths and three areas for development; it could be two, four or even five. The identification of the number three is to offer a starting point and to encourage balance by identifying the same number of strengths and areas for development.

Individual teachers can choose to either write the targeted outcome as part of the meeting or complete this in draft and share it with the learner and their family over the next few days. I would always encourage teachers to write targeted outcomes with the learner and the family, but I am aware that sometimes the wording takes time and if a teacher is still gaining confidence with this way of working, they may want a little more thinking time. It is essential that the ABC elements are co-produced with the learner and their family, so the teacher should agree with the learner and family the priority areas for development or attributes (A) to be worked on this half term and ask the learner and their family member what they think their baseline or starting point is (B). After all the learner knows themselves the best! Similarly, it is essential that all contribute to the identification of the anticipated change that is aimed for. If the teacher wants a little more time to write the 'do' element (D) of the targeted outcome, where they will define the details of the "I want you to do this, SO YOU CAN do that" part of the targeted outcome, this can be shared later. Of course, asking the learner and their family for their thoughts about actions that could help them is essential but the formal wording of the targeted outcome can be returned to.

How we record this information is also significant in terms of promoting participation of learners with the APDR cycle. Many of us now use electronic formats such as provision map which can be a tremendous tool for SENCOs. But ensuring meaningful access to the ABC-D element of the process is vital for the learner and their family. It is not a case of needing to duplicate information but rather looking to see how we can assimilate both requirements. For example, various colleagues have discussed the potential of integrating a printable sheet in the shape of a bookmark within their learning plans. The advantage being that the information is still only recorded once but specific elements are extracted for use by the learner. Although not a bookmark, the example learning plan provided in this chapter includes an APDR format where the third page can be printed on its own, folded and glued to create a targeted outcome 'pyramid' or

Toblerone! This could be kept on the learner's desk as a prompt and reminder of what they are working on, or for older students, this could be adapted to include a summary sheet that could be printed for a blazer pocket. The intent is that the example in the sample learning plan that follows could be useful as a starting point, but as always adopt or adapt this idea so that it works within your existing formats. Unless of course you dislike your existing formats, in which case I would encourage you to think again and work with staff, learners and families to develop a more user-friendly version.

My Learning Plan

Name: Ajay Davis

Age: 7 years old

Class/year group: Willow Class/Year 3

Birthday: 12-4-18

Plan completed with: Ms Carter (teacher), Mrs Davis (Mum) and me

Date: 22-1-25

About Me

Who I live with: Mum, Stephen and my brother Arthur, 5 years old. I see Dad and Chloe every other weekend.

Things I like: I like Lego, climbing trees and playing Minecraft.

What I find tricky: Maths, remembering things and keeping still.

I'd like to be good at: Maths and scoring goals in football.

My strengths:
– Creativity – making things – I have made lots of great Lego models and I enjoy making junk models.
– Compassion – friendships – I have lots of friends and enjoy playing games at break and lunchtimes.
– Co-ordination – writing – I am able to form letters neatly and I like writing, drawing and colouring.

Assess

My teacher noticed that:	My family noticed that:	I noticed that:
• I blurt out ideas and thoughts • I find it hard to remember things • I find it hard to describe my feelings	• I am always on the go and call out a lot • I need to be told things lots of times • I throw things when I am cross	• I have lots of thoughts • I can never remember what to do • Not sure

Plan: Adjustments/support/resources

In class my teacher will:	In class I will:
• Let me sit at the front • Check out what I remember at the start of a lesson • Give me picture cards of feelings	• Try to whisper my ideas • Ask for help if I can't remember • Use the picture cards to keep an eye on my feelings

Plan: Intervention

My teacher will make sure I can take part in all learning activities and in addition will:

1. Remind me to try to hold my ideas.
2. Get me to repeat work instructions and to use pictures and checklists to help me.
3. Teach me words that describe feelings and help me to notice my own feelings.

Do

Ajay's targeted outcomes printable pyramid

A – Area for development/Attribute	B – Baseline	C – Change	D – Do
Control – Impulsivity I have lots of ideas and thoughts that burst out of me!	The teacher counted that I called out 18 times in ten minutes.	I will try to hold some of my thoughts so when the teacher counts next time, I will only call out nine times in ten minutes.	I will play musical statues and 'hold it' games with Mrs Jones and three other children twice a week at lunchtime SO I CAN practice holding my words and actions.

A – Area for development/Attribute	B – Baseline	C – Change	D – Do
Cognition – Working memory I listen but I can't always remember what has been said.	I can remember one thing at a time.	I want to remember two things that are said to me.	I will work with Mr Jones and four friends to play memory games SO I CAN see if this helps me remember two things in the classroom.

A – Area for development/Attribute	B – Baseline	C – Change	D – Do
Communication – Expressive Vocabulary I find it hard to think of some words to say, especially about my feelings.	I stay quiet when I am asked how I feel, or I shrug my shoulders.	I want to use words to describe when I feel happy, sad, worried, excited or unsure.	I will work with Mrs Jones and three friends to look at pictures and words that describe feelings SO I CAN use these words or pictures when I am asked how I feel.

Review

My teacher noticed that:	My family noticed that:	I noticed that:

Assess: My next steps are:

Plan: Adjustments/support/resources

In class my teacher will:	In class I will:

Plan: Intervention

My teacher will make sure I can take part in all learning activities and, in addition, will:

Ajay's targeted outcomes printable pyramid

Do –

A – Area for development/Attribute	B – Baseline	C – Change	D – Do

A – Area for development/Attribute	B – Baseline	C – Change	D – Do

A – Area for development/Attribute	B – Baseline	C – Change	D – Do

Review

My teacher noticed that:	My family noticed that:	I noticed that:

Assess: My next steps are:

Plan: Adjustments/support/resources

In class my teacher will:	In class I will:

Plan: Intervention

My teacher will make sure I can take part in all learning activities and, in addition will:

My learning plan

Photo

Name:

Age: Birthday:

Class/year group: Plan completed with:

About me   Date:

Who I live with:

Things I like:

What I find tricky:

I'd like to be good at:

My strengths:

Assess

My teacher noticed that:	My family noticed that:	I noticed that:

Plan: Adjustments/support/resources

In class my teacher will:	In class I will:

Plan: Intervention

My teacher will make sure I can take part in all learning activities and, in addition will:

My targeted outcomes printable pyramid

Do

A – Area for development/ Attribute	B – Baseline	C – Change	D – Do

A – Area for development/ Attribute	B – Baseline	C – Change	D – Do

A – Area for development/ Attribute	B – Baseline	C – Change	D – Do

Review

My teacher noticed that:	My family noticed that:	I noticed that:

Assess: My next steps are:

Plan: Adjustments/support/resources

In class my teacher will:	In class I will:

Plan: Intervention

My teacher will make sure I can take part in all learning activities and, in addition, will:

My targeted outcomes printable pyramid:

Do –

A – Area for development/ Attribute	B – Baseline	C – Change	D – Do

A – Area for development/ Attribute	B – Baseline	C – Change	D – Do

A – Area for development/ Attribute	B – Baseline	C – Change	D – Do

Review

My teacher noticed that:	My family noticed that:	I noticed that:

Assess: My next steps are:

Plan: Adjustments/support/resources

In class my teacher will:	In class I will:

Plan: Intervention

My teacher will make sure I can take part in all learning activities and, in addition will:

5. Using the 7 Cs Progress Tracker

Capturing small steps of progress can be challenging. Demonstrating improvements with learning attributes such as anxiety management, self-regulation, confidence or self-esteem can be difficult. These skills are often considered to be 'soft' rather than 'hard', which is ironic because actually these are incredibly hard to teach, learn and apply, yet so many of our staff and learners are doing exactly this. Often our traditional system of assessment can be dismissive of such skills, even though the absence of these skills can, for many, become a significant barrier to the curriculum. It was for this reason that the 7 Cs Progress Tracker was written. If you have seen this resource, you will know that the progress tracker consists of a rating scale to support teacher assessment of starting points and for use to demonstrate progress relative to each starting point. This has been welcomed by many SENCOs and SEN Practitioners and is deemed a useful tool for SEND leadership as it really can help to evidence-base an individual learner's progress 'journey'. That said, it should be used with caution.

The reason for promoting caution relates to the risk of shifting intent. **The Progress Tracker should never become the targeted outcome itself.** We should never aspire for a learner to 'become a 5' as this, in itself, is nonsense. We should describe our aspiration, defining what this will look like for the learner, and then map this against the Progress Tracker at specific intervals to help inform our monitoring of the effectiveness of our provision. For example, within cognition: working memory in the Progress Tracker, emerging 1–3 describes a learner as having "small capacity so difficulties holding or retaining one or two pieces of information. Finds remembering instructions tricky and following requests". The evolving 4–6 descriptor says, "small to medium capacity. Able to hold 2–3-part instructions but loses details tending to remember general elements or will fill in gaps". The tracker only has meaning if the teacher's assessment of the lived experience of the learner includes a description of what is seen rather than simply promoting a change of number from 2 to 4.

Caution is also required to ensure realistic and consistent teacher assessment using the Progress Tracker. It is highly unlikely that a learner will move from rating scale 2 to 7 within half a term! Many learning attributes are complex and challenging to shift. They need time and rehearsal to either build capacity or develop greater efficiency in using existing capacity. For example, working memory changes may result from the enhancement of the efficiency of the learner in using their working memory and/or support strategies, rather than increasing the capacity itself. Once again, it is essential that we support staff to value the Progress Tracker as a best fit and not view it as a curriculum syllabus and to accept that not every learning attribute for every learner (child or adult) can or should become a 10 or be enhanced! We each have an individual learning profile with strengths and areas for development. We are not striving to 'race' to enhance all attributes for everyone, but rather, to promote skill development in areas that are limiting curriculum access. These barriers are the focus of our collaborative targeted outcomes. As you monitor and quality assure samples of APDRs, keep an eye on the use of the Progress Tracker to ensure that it is being used to capture progress and not to become the provision itself.

6. Quality assurance

The practical management of quality assurance (QA) activities starts and finishes with the protection of time. It is as simple and as complex as that! Time is, of course, a limited resource so investing it wisely is essential. The annual strategic planner introduced in Chapter 3, along with the resources within the SEND QA Toolkit, can help to aspire for the protection and organisation of QA time. Inevitably the annual strategic planner will become the plan that you 'deviate from' as events change rapidly in schools. But reflect this in your plan. It will be incredibly useful to track the actual time that is available for QA activities against your plan so you can share this with other senior leaders, revealing the need for a more distributed approach to QA time if your time continues to be eroded. This prospect in itself may encourage collegiate protection of your time (to avoid the distribution of tasks to other leaders) or indeed build capacity for QA activities by distributing tasks, which ultimately is a rare win-win scenario! In reality, the operational demands of the SENCO role often exceed the available time, but without strategic tasks such as planning, monitoring via quality assurance and evaluation, the role will remain reactive with a risk of feeling increasingly overwhelming with less impact. **Quality assurance is the difference between coordinating SEND and the leadership of SEND.**

Once time is protected and activities are distributed and underway, focus on evaluating the information you are gathering. What is the information telling you? Is this as you expected? What are the implications and next steps? Use the information you gather to inform the next cycle of intent, implementation and impact of the SEND system. Where possible, build in regular short opportunities for QA activities as 'little but often' really is the most effective management approach. Also seek to involve others and ensure that information is fed back to senior leaders and governors or trustees. When time allows re-read Chapter 3 of this book and adopt or adapt the SEND QA Toolkit so you have a recording pack 'ready' to go. And of course, don't forget to drag and drop information into your portfolio of evidence as an ongoing process so that you have evaluative evidence of the intent, implementation and impact of the SEND system in your setting.

7. The adoption of a strengths-based approach

The 7 Cs Learning Portfolio is a strength-based framework and promotes the identification and utilisation of learner strengths. It attempts to bring balance to SEND identification, as instead of just identifying barriers to learning, strengths are identified and celebrated alongside areas for development. In real terms, teachers are encouraged to identify three strengths and three areas for development as part of the assess, plan, do and review cycle. However, a strengths-based approach involves more than this. The origins of strengths-based practice links to person centred approaches within humanistic psychology. Carl Rogers and a number of other Psychologists in the 1940s were dissatisfied with the perspectives used in counselling so introduced 'client centred therapy'. The shift in emphasis was that the client was seen as an active participant in the counselling process. This approach evolved and was adopted in social work and transitioned into education as person centred approaches. References to person centred approaches were included in the SEND Code of Practice in 2014 and the current revised version of 2015. Positivepsychology.com state that:

> With its foundation in social work, the strengths-based approach is a 'work practice theory' that focuses on an individual's self-determination and strength (McCashen, 2005). This type of approach builds on clients strengths, seeing them as resourceful and resilient when they are in adverse conditions. It is also client led and centred on outcomes, getting people to affect change in themselves. The strengths-based approach allows a person to see themselves at their best – the value they bring by just being themselves. They are encouraged to capitalise on their strengths rather than focus on negative characteristics.

Encouraging learners to see themselves at their best and to recognise the values they bring, just by being themselves, is a central construct of the Essential SENCO Toolkit. From this perspective, learning and growth, confidence and resiliency will be optimised. Strengths-based SEND leadership will celebrate the individuation of all and maximise the opportunities for diverse collaboration. Assimilating the nine principles of a strengths-based approach, as described by Hammond in 2010, encourages a dynamic and robust approach to leadership. Hammond (2010) identified nine guiding principles as the foundation of a strengths-based approach. These are:

1. A belief that everyone is unique and it is this uniqueness that helps them evolve and progress along their journey.
2. What is given attention or focus becomes what the client strives for and becomes their reality.
3. Language creates our reality so we must be careful of our words and language.
4. Acceptance of change is essential as everything evolves and changes.
5. Support others as authentically as possible.
6. The client is the storyteller of their own story.
7. Build upon what you know and experience in order to dream of the future.
8. Capacity building needs to be flexible.
9. Be collaborative, adaptive and value differences.

The implication of this set of principles is that to be strengths-based, we need to consider how we:

- Promote learner uniqueness and celebrate difference.
- Empower learners to comment on their lived experiences, hopes, dreams and aspirations.
- Create space and time for expression and collaboration.
- Demonstrate our belief in learner capacity.
- Show curiosity and empathy.
- Listen.
- Remain flexible and genuinely collaborative.

This approach impacts on the policy, practice and culture of our settings which is why it is an essential tool for leadership. Taking time to reflect on the implication of this in practice will help to extend your strengths-based approach beyond simply identifying three strengths and three areas for development. Evaluating your school or settings cultural expectations, language and system flexibility could be a useful starting point. Maryanne Peters, SENDCO and DSL at Diss Primary Academy Partnership and Scole CE Primary Academy, has found:

> This approach places the child's strengths at the forefront. It encompasses the child, their family and the school together in a flexible document, which can be adapted to suit individual needs.

8. Setting up a SEND Portfolio of Evidence

The SEND Portfolio of Evidence as described in Chapter 5, was written to aid the practical management of SEND systems. It is simply an electronic framework for holding evidence and examples of practice. The starting point is to create electronic folders that correlate to the 12 sections of the SEND review audit evaluation tool. Information can then be dragged and dropped into each section to enable the immediate identification of existing evidence and any gaps in evidence. If there are gaps in evidence, use this knowledge to inform next steps and undertake relevant actions.

The key to the SEND Portfolio of Evidence is to populate the folders with evidence that already exists, rather than attempting to create new or duplicated responses. View the portfolio as a working 'scrapbook' where you can add copies of referrals, observation records or APDR paperwork that already exists as part of your evidence gathering about the SEND system. That way, the information can be shared with other senior leaders, governors, Trust leads, LA officers or Ofsted as the need arises. It can also help to fine tune your own sense of strengths and areas for development regarding the evidence available. It is essential that the portfolio is reviewed regularly and updated. Updates will involve the deletion or replacement of information, otherwise the portfolio will lose its relevance and you will not be able to access the information quickly. Maintaining the portfolio of evidence requires the courage to delete and to replace documents, remembering of course, that the portfolio itself holds copies of existing documents, and really is simply an annual portal for evidence exploration. Individual records will still build over time, but you may just include the most recent set of APDR cycles for that year. Ultimately, it is your portfolio so you will find the best way of managing the information, but be clear of purpose, and remember the rationale for the evidence.

9. Evaluating the SEND system from a learner's perspective

The importance of exploring the SEND system from the lens of a learner, was outlined in Chapter 6, but how can you go about achieving this? A starting point is either case sampling or utilising the pupil perspective form within learning walks and other QA tasks. This can be most effective when shared across the leadership team as all leaders will be focused on the 'so what' aspect of SEND quality assurance. A pupil perspective evaluation is a powerful reminder of the purpose or intent of the SEND system and these tools can aid the collation of evidence and promote conversations.

Practical management of the necessary triangulation of these activities would include establishing a regular learner forum where questions are shared and explored. Some SENCOs have combined learner focus groups with shared hot chocolate, or squash and biscuit/fruit meetings. But as always, it is essential to be prepared to hear the answers to questions, even if the answers are not as expected or desired. **SEND leadership is not about searching for the 'correct' answer to questions, but the adoption of curiosity and reflection which will inform meaningful evaluation. Eliciting the views of learners will give you the insight that is required to fully understand your SEND systems.**

10. The implementation of EHCPs

As we know, it can take a long time to receive an EHCP for a learner, so how do we practically manage the use and implementation of an EHCP when it has finally been issued? How useful is the plan for the learner themselves? Their family? Or the teacher? How accessible is the information within the plan and how is it integrated into the personalised learning opportunities for that individual? When the Code of Practice for SEN was first published in 1994, the system involved a five staged linear approach whereby stage 1 involved monitoring and stage 2 required action in school. Stage 3 involved action in school informed by outside agencies and stage 4 was the point at which a statutory assessment was underway. Stage 5 was when a Statement of Special Educational Needs was in place. When the Statement was finalised, schools working with the learner's family and other professionals known to the learner, had three months to complete a statement implementation plan. This was a formal opportunity to consider how the statement targets would be implemented in school. The advantage of the Statement implementation plan was the coming together of all those working with the learner in order to share ideas and practical suggestions for implementing the requirements of the Statement. Fast forward 30 years and several versions of the Code of Practice later and there is now no longer any protected time for collaborative action planning regarding the implementation of the Education, Health and Care Plan. Instead, schools are often 'left' to interpret what can at times be fairly ambiguous learning outcomes. Unless of course, you instigate your own system for EHCP implementation planning? The example below contains a simple EHCP implementation planning form intended to help identify priority barriers and actions. The purpose being to support teacher access to these individual plans and to extend the opportunity of an SEN support conversation to those families of learners with an EHCP. The next time you receive an EHCP for a learner, consider inviting all those that know the learner, the learner themselves and their family alongside the teacher, TA and yourself, and agree an EHCP implementation strategy. The purpose being to aid understanding, evoke a sharing of knowledge and ideas and to build collaborative ambition for the learner based on immediate priorities outlined in the plan.

EHCP implementation plan

Learner name:
Date:
Completed by:

Strengths:

Barriers to learning:

Outcomes from EHCP:

1.

2.

3.

4.

5.

6.

7.

8.

9.

10.

Priority actions:
In school:

At home or out and about:

Additional support or information:

Interim review date

Reflections

- The Essential SENCO Toolkit contains an extensive range of approaches that can support SEND leadership, but where is your starting point? The 7 Cs Learning Portfolio? The 4 Functions of Learning Support? Targeted outcomes? Strengths-based inclusive school culture?
- What does the SEND system do well? What needs to improve?
- How can you practically manage your next steps with this toolkit?

Actions to consider

- Re-read the titles of the ten themes within this chapter. Which three resonate the most with you?
- Choose one of the these themes as a starting point for action and share the theme with other senior leaders.
- Talk to learners themselves about their lived experiences in school, ask them to identify three strengths and three areas for school development.

8. CPD

A key construct of the Essential SENCO toolkit is the importance of ongoing Continued Professional Development (CPD). The connecting 7 Cs, 7 Ps and 7 Ds hexagons were not coincidental, but an intentional method of reinforcing the centrality of ongoing continued professional development. This is because CPD protects time for reflection, evaluation and refinement. It should help to sustain motivation and inspiration and promote a connection with values and purpose. This in turn improves the quality of teaching and learning opportunities, thus boosting the likelihood of positive outcomes for all learners. CPD is a fundamental right and requirement of the teaching profession. The Education Endowment Foundation, in their guidance report on effective professional development, write:

> PD may take a variety of different meanings in different contexts …we define teacher professional development as structured and facilitated activity for teachers intended to increase their teaching ability.
>
> *(EEF Effective Professional Development, page 7)*

Within their guidance report, they recommend:

1. When designing and selecting professional development, focus on the mechanisms.
2. Ensure that professional development effectively builds knowledge, motivates staff, develops teaching techniques and embeds practice.
3. Implement professional development programmes with care, taking into consideration the context and needs of the school.

Similarly, the Health Care Professionals Council (HCPC) define CPD as:

> CPD is the way in which you continue to learn and develop throughout your career so you keep your skills and knowledge up to date and are able to practise safely and effectively. CPD is not only formal courses but any activity from which you learn and develop.
>
> *(page 4)*

DOI: 10.4324/9781003408994-9

And, of course, within education we are consistently involved in activities in which we learn and develop. **As leaders of SEND, CPD opportunities represent an essential tool for improved intent, implementation and impact of SEND systems.** By ensuring the relevance and effectiveness of structured and facilitated activities for staff, you have the potential to build knowledge and motivation and further advance teaching techniques. The selection of effective activities and development themes is an essential part of SEND leadership and needs to emerge from the information elicited as part of your monitoring, quality assurance and planning. The Teacher's Standards requires all teachers to be able to "adapt teaching to respond to the strengths and needs of all pupils". Teacher Standard number 5 includes the requirement to know when and how to differentiate; to have a secure understanding of factors that can inhibit learning and how to overcome these; to be able to demonstrate an awareness of the physical, social and intellectual development of children and how to adapt teaching to support pupils; and to have a clear understanding of the needs of pupils, including those with SEND, those of high ability and those with English as an additional language and be able to use and evaluate distinctive teaching approaches to engage and support them. SEND leaders working with other senior leaders will be influential in securing these training opportunities. But what does this look like?

The DfE commissioned Ofsted to undertake an independent review of teachers' professional development in schools, which resulted in the publication of two research papers: "Independent Review of Teachers' Professional Development in Schools Phase 1 Findings" (May 2023) and "Independent Review of Teachers' Professional Development in Schools Phase 2 Findings" (May 2024). They reported that "high quality professional development that improves teachers' knowledge, practice and confidence can have a positive impact on pupils' outcomes". They also found that this can increase teacher satisfaction about their roles and increase the likelihood that staff will remain in their jobs. The Phase 1 report concluded that, on the whole, Early Careers Teachers (ECTs) and staff accessing NPQs were very positive about their CPD opportunities. However, they identified several barriers that prevented more experienced teachers from receiving sufficient development opportunities. This prompted further research as part of the Phase 2 study, which replicated the finding that ECTs and those studying for NPQs were generally more positive about the quality of their training and development opportunities. In contrast, experienced and part-time teachers said they were not getting a high-quality teacher development offer. Instead, this was often described as "piecemeal and not strategically planned". Often training priorities were deemed to focus on short-term "crisis management" themes and preparation for Ofsted rather than the enhancement of knowledge and skills.

In contrast, where CPD was deemed effective, there was evidence of long-term strategic planning with staff following a coherent programme of development. Staff had access to a menu of formal and informal development opportunities which led to increases in confidence, skills and capacity to respond to emerging needs in schools. Ofsted concluded that there is no "one size fits all" approach, and strong teacher development often involved a range of opportunities that were both internally and externally sourced and enabled teachers to fulfil individual learning goals as well as to meet the whole school contextual priorities.

This is a view also presented by Enser and Enser (2021) in their book *The CPD Curriculum*. They quote the DfE Standard for Teachers' Professional Development (July 2016) by writing:

> The design of high-quality professional development is as complex a discipline as the design of high-quality teaching. It requires the planning of programmes of connected activities with clarity about intended outcomes, and evaluation.
>
> *(page 23)*

With this in mind, SENCOs and SEN Practitioners may wish to create and contribute to an annual CPD programme that contains a range of bespoke SEND themed CPD opportunities. However, if the design of high-quality professional development is as complex a discipline as the design of high-quality teaching, our immediate step when planning SEND themed CPD opportunities is to review our baseline or starting point for staff. The SEND-themed CPD Staff Audit contains a short set of questions for staff to use to evaluate their confidence with SEND. The questions relate to the details of the teacher standards number 5 and SEND theme and CPD modality preferences. As always, you are encouraged to adopt or adapt these questions to meet your needs. You may already use an effective teacher CPD audit or questionnaire and if this provides you with clarity of starting point and a baseline to plan your SEND themed CPD activities then carry on with that model. If not, perhaps try this one and evaluate the relevance of information gathered.

SEND-themed CPD Staff Audit

	Yes	No	Sometimes
I feel confident differentiating learning tasks for all learners with SEND			
I use a range of adaptive teaching approaches to ensure that my lessons are accessible to all			
I have a secure understanding of how a range of factors can inhibit learning and how best to overcome these			
I demonstrate an awareness of the physical, social and intellectual development of learners and know how to adapt teaching to support all			
I have a clear understanding of the needs of all pupils, including those with SEND, and can use and evaluate distinctive teaching approaches to engage them			

I would like training on:

	Yes	No	Maybe
Using SEND systems – SEN support, reviews, annual reviews, EHCPs			
Supporting cognition and learning – working memory, processing, dyslexia, dyscalculia			
Supporting communication and interaction – autism, ADHD, Speech and Language			
Supporting SEMH – anxiety, self-regulation, impulsivity, attachment			
Supporting physical/sensory – dyspraxia, cerebral palsy, Down syndrome, sensory processing			

The modality of CPD learning I prefer is:

	Yes	No	Sometimes
Trainer led			
E-Learning			
Workshop/group			
Consultation			
Self-directed			

I feel confident in my understanding of SEND in relation to:

I would like to know more about:

I anticipate that this would improve my practice in the following ways:

The information gathered from the staff audit can help to identify key priorities and provide evidence of the baseline skills of staff. As is associated with the 'day job' of teaching, you will of course have a spectrum of expertise and confidence. SEND-themed CPD task priorities will need to offer personalisation and adaptive teaching elements. To fulfil this requirement, it can be useful to consider options both in terms of the modality of delivery and content. With regard to the modality of delivery, you might consider providing activities that are:

- Trainer led
- E-learning
- Workshop or small group
- Consultation
- Self-directed

SEND themed CPD content will of course vary according to the priorities identified by staff and the whole-school priorities written within your school development plan, as well as information gathered from your annual provision mapping process. This includes the arrival of learners with specific learning needs and/or the findings of your annual quality assurance and monitoring. In addition to this, you may also want to consider the anticipated impact or outcomes of SEND-themed CPD opportunities. A method for evaluating impact and measuring outcomes is to define the anticipated impact of the session. The HCPC encourages an evaluation of purpose regarding the 'what, why, how, when and where' of the information. For example, is the anticipated impact linked to an increase in the following areas:

1. **Knowledge and information** – is the purpose of the activity to enhance 'what' is known and understood?
2. **Rationale and understanding** – is the purpose of the activity to promote greater clarity and consistency regarding the 'why' of something?
3. **Process, procedural and practical** – is the purpose of the activity to promote a shared understanding of the 'how'?
4. **Implementation** – is the purpose of the activity to guide understanding regarding the 'when' of use?
5. **Context** – is the purpose of the activity to promote understanding of the 'where' that this should be used?

With this framework, leaders can plan a diverse and personalised CPD programme and staff engaging with this can also evaluate the impact and relevance.

The SEND-themed CPD activity planning tool can be used to help populate ideas and themes across each of the modalities of learning and according to outcomes. You may choose to simply record activity ideas within the relevant sections of the grid and then use these to inform the completion of the SEND-themed CPD Activity Annual Planner template. An example is also provided to help illustrate the potential application of this tool. So, when time allows, have a look at these templates and consider whether they could be adopted or adapted for your setting.

SEND CPD Activity Planning Tool – Year:

	Knowledge and Information (What)	Rationale and Understanding (Why)	Process, Procedural and Practical (How)	Implementation (When)	Contextual (Where)
Trainer led					
E-learning					
Workshop					
Consultation					
Self-directed					

My SEND CPD Summary Record – Name:

	Knowledge and Information (What)	Rationale and Understanding (Why)	Process, Procedural and Practical (How)	Implementation (When)	Contextual (Where)
Trainer led					
E-learning					
Workshop					
Consultation					
Self-directed					

SEND CPD Activity – School Planner

Academic Year:

What are we doing?	Why this and not something else? (SIDP and or provision mapping)	How will it be delivered? (modality)	Who will take part?	When will this take place?	Who will facilitate?	How much will it cost?	Impact and follow up?

SEND CPD Activity Planner – Willow Tree Primary Academy Annual Planner

Academic Year: 2024–2025: Autumn 2024

What are we doing?	Why this and not something else? (SIDP and or provision mapping)	How will it be delivered? (modality)	Who will take part?	When will this take place?	Who will facilitate?	How much will it cost?	Impact and follow up?
Understanding Autism – whole school training day	SIDP priority emerged from increased numbers of new pupils with autism.	Trainer Led and Workshops	All staff – Teachers, Co-Educators, Midday Assistants, Clerical and Caretaking.	25-10-24 Inset Day.	Keynote Speaker: Claire Jordan.	£600	
TA Training on Coaching for Kids.	SIDP priority: improving the quality of support and questioning used by learning mentors.	Workshops	All co-educators, SENCO, SEN governor.	Ternly training within monthly team meeting session: 4-1-25 and 5-5-25.	SENCO, using the resources from "Life Coaching for Kids" by Nikki Giant.	No additional costs beyond the purchase price of the book (£19).	
Can the use of metacognitive questioning improve independent learning?	SIDP priority: improving learning and independence.	Trainer led and Workshop	Teaching staff	Twilight 22-11-24 Plus three themed staff meetings as follow up: 29-11-24, 5-2-25, 8-5-25	EP to lead Twilight Deputy head and SENCO facilitate staff meetings	£350 EP cost	

What are we doing?	Why this and not something else? (SIDP and or provision mapping)	How will it be delivered? (modality)	Who will take part?	When will this take place?	Who will facilitate?	How much will it cost?	Impact and follow up?
"Life Coaching for Kids" by Nikki Giant is the Autumn term book for the Teacher book club	Recommended by EP for practical resources and accessible theory on coaching approaches.	Self-directed	Book club identifies a book that every teacher will read within a term.	Six copies available from 3-9-24. The expectation is that will be read and passed on by half term.	SENCO will launch at the staff meeting on 3-9-24 and allocate the initial six copies, and launch the exchange on 25-10-24.	Six copies of book purchased (£19 × 6 = £114)	

These resources are intended to support the process of SEND-themed CPD planning as a leadership tool. Enser and Enser (2021) identify similarities between CPD planning and the creation of a jigsaw puzzle. They write:

> When we begin to work on a jigsaw puzzle, we start by looking at the big picture on the front of the box. This is the vision which we have for our overall school improvement and as such needs to be shared and agreed with all. We are all working together to create this image and we need a clear understanding of what our ideal school looks like.
>
> *(page 30)*

This is also true when we focus on themes for SEND, as, to have any relevance and impact, SEND-themed CPD needs to be an integral part of whole-school planning and improvement. Although our tools in this chapter have focused on SEND themes for CPD specifically, they are, of course, an integral part of CPD and whole-school improvement in general. SEND-themed CPD is not a separate jigsaw, but rather an integrated element of the whole-school picture. In the same way as learners with SEND should not be an 'add-on' to existing systems, as they are an integral part of the whole school community, CPD with SEND themes should be an integral part of whole-school development planning.

All of us engaging with CPD activities have a responsibility to record and evaluate the impact on practice. To support this process you may wish to share the 'My CPD Record' form with staff and/or use this to capture your own activities and perceived impact. You will notice that it includes an opportunity to capture the modality and outcome of each activity, as well as encouraging professional reflection on impact, evaluation and action planning. The template is included along with a completed example for consideration. The intent of its inclusion here is to encourage a professional conversation with staff about the nature of CPD records and planning in order to promote greater efficacy and ownership of this issue.

My CPD Record

Name:
School:
Ranked outcomes:
1 = Knowledge and information (What?) 2 = Rationale and understanding (Why?) 3 = Process, procedural and practical (How?) 4 = Implementation (When?) 5 = Context (Where?)

Date of Activity	Name of Activity	Trainer Led	E-Learning	Workshop	Consultation	Self-Directed	Ranked Outcome	Perceived Impact, Evaluation and Action Planning

My CPD Record

Name: Judith Carter
School: Willow Tree Primary Academy
Ranked outcomes:
1 = Knowledge and information (What?) 2 = Rationale and understanding (Why?) 3 = Process, procedural and practical (How?)
4 = Implementation (When?) 5 = Context (Where?)

Date of Activity	Name of Activity	Trainer Led	E-Learning	Workshop	Consultation	Self-Directed	Ranked Outcome	Perceived Impact, Evaluation and Action Planning
17-9-24	SENCO/LA forum – LA updates two hour twilight	x					1, 3 = 4	Update on EHC needs assessment – new form. Action: review Local Offer and read revised criteria for EHC needs referral
5-10-24	Essential SENCO Network – 2.5 hours, news and two CPD taster sessions: Dyslexia and metacognition	x		x			1, 2, 3 = 6	Really useful session, specifically Metacognition planning. Types of questioning will be shared at staff meeting
25-10-24	Staff inset: Understanding Autism – full day	x		x			1, 2, 3, 4, 5 = 15	Morning input from the speaker gave useful insight. In the afternoon session, staff agreed on revised adjustments to support pupils with autism in school.
12-11-24	"Life Coaching for Kids" by Nikki Giant					x	1, 2, 3 = 6	Identified useful resources from this book. Planning LSA training using materials.
4-1-25	LSA training on life coaching			x			1, 2, 3, 4, 5 = 15	Consistent language of coaching now established with LSA team with a pack of materials for application. Will monitor in four weeks.

CPD is an essential leadership tool. For leaders of SEND, maximising these opportunities can enhance the potential for development and change. It sits at the heart of quality assurance, as it will both inform what you see 'now' and will shape what you see 'next' regarding staff performance, knowledge and skills and it is the vehicle for school improvement. Enser and Enser (2021) write:

> We hope that anyone who is reading this will now agree that CPD should sit at the centre of a school leader's thoughts whenever they are considering how their school should move forward. If they can get CPD right, then they will grow expert teachings in their own schools and mitigate the system-wide problem with staff retention. These expert teachers will then be better able to lead on their own development and so they will end up with a self-improving system. All of this will lead to better pupil outcomes, by any measure.

Reflections

- What is your contribution to CPD planning at a whole school and SEND themed level?
- How strategic are SEND-themed CPD activities?
- What influences the choice of nominated SEND-themed CPD activities?
- Do you currently use an annual skills audit to baseline staff views? Or identify themes from provision mapping and/or quality assurance and monitoring?
- Can you demonstrate the anticipated and actual impact of SEND-themed CPD activities?
- Do you and other staff and leaders 'own' your individual record of your CPD activities or is this recorded elsewhere? Are there merits in individual ownership and evaluation?

Actions to consider

- Share the staff SEND-themed CPD audit from this chapter and review the findings. Are there any surprises in these or are the views expressed as expected?
- Review the SEND-themed CPD activity planning tool and attempt to 'plot' activities within each of the categories and modalities for learning. Are there any patterns to this?
- Work with other senior leaders to develop an annual SEND-themed CPD planner and 'notice' whether this enhances the relevance and impact of activity choices.

9. SEND LEADership

Leadership and management are often used interchangeably but are different activities. A leader may manage, but not all managers will lead. The focus of this book has been to promote your leadership capacity as well as to support the coordination or management of SEND throughout your setting. The distinction is that as leaders, you will work with others to determine the intent of the SEND system, you will work with others and support them to implement the SEND system, and you will review the impact or effectiveness of this in practice. Roedel (2021) writes:

> Leadership and management are not the same things so its important to be able to understand the difference. Management is more about managing the day-to-day operations of a business or team. Leadership, however, is ensuring that others are bought into a shared vision and that everyone is working together as a team to achieve those goals.
>
> *(page 36)*

Establishing a shared vision and ensuring cohesive collaboration and working together is ultimately about clarity of intent and implementation. The Essential SENCO Toolkit can support you to define and refine your approach to SEND leadership. As Paul A. Wyatt describes in his book *How to Lead for Daring New Leaders* (2022) there are many published styles of leadership, originating from Kurt Lewin in the 1930s, who, working with a team of psychologists and researchers, sought to define three distinct styles. Firstly, an autocratic leader, who dictates by a command and control model of order to action. Secondly, a laissez-faire model evidenced by a lack of control and responsibility,and characterised by freedom and constant need for guidance. And thirdly there is a more democratic style. Over the years these definitions have evolved and developed, and Wyatt (2022) identifies four intentional styles of leadership: transactional, servant, laissez-faire and transformational.

> Transactional leadership relies on guidelines, rules, parameters and standards of performance. It has a fairly rigid approach with an explicit 'bottom line'.

DOI: 10.4324/9781003408994-10

The servant model of leadership, in comparison focuses on what the leader can do for the followers. This includes the provision of assistance, encouragement and resources. The laissez-faire model promotes freedom and seeks to promote creativity and empowerment. And the transformational leader, according to Wyatt (2022), is a storyteller, relying on communication and self-evaluation with an ongoing belief in self-improvement. The literature in this area clearly shows that there are a multitude of leadership models and styles with varying degrees of relevance and appropriateness for SENCOs and SEN Practitioners. And although the theme of this book is SEND leadership, instead of focusing on styles of leadership, the focus here will shift to SEND LEADership principles as these principles are deemed most relevant to informing leadership practice. The change in spelling is intentional and is designed to promote a useful summary of four principles of SEND leadership that are present throughout the Essential SENCO Toolkit.

The four principles of SEND LEADership are offered as prompts for evaluation and to support development planning and are:

L = Language

E = Empowerment

A = Ambition

D = Deliberateness

Language

Establishing a shared language of SEND within a community such as a school or academy is vital. As we explored in Chapter 1, ensuring that all staff, learners and their families have the same understanding of SEN, SEND and medical needs is essential. Along with a shared understanding of the rationale for identification and the expectations of provision or action with intent. Related to this is the importance of a strengths-based language and a valuing of difference. As part of your evaluation, you may reflect on whether all adults acknowledge and celebrate the strengths of all learners, including those with SEND? Is there consistency with the avoidance of deficit language or the description 'SEND learners' instead of learners with SEND? Does your language value progress relative to starting points, avoiding terms such as falling behind, underachieving, needs to catch up? As part of your inclusive culture, do you value the contribution of all?

A shared and consistent language is also essential for our communication with children, young people and their families. But how accessible are our conversations, policies and procedures? Do they evoke collaboration and equality? Do we have a shared strengths-based language that describes learning attributes, personal qualities and characteristics? Are learners and families able to share their reflections, experiences and development suggestions with us?

Clarity of language is an essential leadership principle, both in terms of promoting consistency but also to enable collaboration and shared direction. Our language is a vehicle for our values. As Hammond (2010) identified when describing the foundation of strengths-based practice, our language creates our reality.

Empowerment

The SEND leadership principle of empowerment perceives the purpose of a SEND system as capacity and confidence building. Both with regards to individual learners, but also building capacity and confidence for families and staff working within the system. As leaders, is it not our role to promote engagement, ownership and development? Empowering learners to understand their learning profile, to identify their strengths and next learning steps increases their likelihood of engagement. Empowering families with the provision of accessible information, knowledge and opportunities for participation will strengthen the SEND system of the setting. As will the empowerment of staff to meet the educational needs of all of their learners, as this will help to advance the quality of teaching and learning. Empowering governors to govern with full knowledge of roles and responsibilities in relation to learners with SEND will enable their active questioning and enhance their capacity to support and challenge. Similarly, empowering TAs to mediate, reinforce, assess and intervene will extend the quality and diversity of learning support available in the setting. And finally, the empowerment of SENCOs as leaders who assess, plan, do and review the SEND system as a whole as well as overseeing the co-ordination of this for individual learners. It is essential that you have time to define SEND intent and time to plan and review its implementation. This will then empower you to evaluate the impact and revise, refine and revisit your intent.

Ambition

Empowerment is connected to ambition. We only seek to empower if we are ambitious as leaders. Ambition in action can look very different for individuals in the same way as equality in its truest sense is about treating people differently in order to access the same opportunities. As leaders of SEND, ambition is an essential tool, both in terms of our aspirations for individual learners, but also for the quality of the teaching and learning within our setting. Similarly, our ambition needs to extend towards families and life outcomes for learners with SEND. We should also be ambitious for the SEND system as a whole. At the time of writing, the SEND system is a self-declared 'broken' system and is awaiting radical change, as SENCOs and SEN Practitioners our ambition should include our ongoing contribution to national and local developments of the system. Too often the system feels as though it is 'done' to us, whether we are staff, parents/carers or learners, so retaining our ambition and contribution to the shaping and development of the system is vital.

All four LEAD principles have a multi-dimensional relevance. They are relevant to our work with individual learners, with families, with staff, with ourselves and the system as a whole. Reviewing SEND LEADership in relation to the individual, the school and the system as a whole is useful in supporting your professional reflections regarding intent, implementation and impact. Is there evidence of ambition within your SEND intent as outlined in your SEN Information Report and policy? Do you 'see' ambition as part of your quality assurance activities evaluating the implementation of SEND systems? And what of the impact? Is there evidence of ambitious outcomes for learners with SEND and their families and staff?

Deliberateness

This principle is a reminder that, even though it may not feel like it, as SEND LEADers, our actions are ours to control. Of course, there are so many things that we cannot change within the SEND system, but our way of reacting, our way of planning and our way of communicating is within our control. The key to SEND LEADership is deliberateness. **Know what you are doing, why you are doing this instead of something else and how you will know it makes a difference.** Ensure that your actions 'match' your intent, they seek to empower and build capacity and retain your ambition for all learners, families and staff. The SENCO and SEN Practitioner role at times will feel highly reactive, and indeed probably is one of the most reactive roles within a school. However, retain control over your reactions and use your intent and ambition to keep you grounded and moving in your preferred direction. The role is incredibly challenging and at times, will feel frustrating and overwhelming and you may feel a disconnect between your intent and your reality. When that happens, deliberately take time to remind yourself of your intent and ambition and empower yourself to try something new. Deliberately 'break' the negative cycle or reaction that is draining you. For me personally, I do this by spending more time with children, as these interactions remind me of why I am trying to do the job I do. Protect time for deliberate curiosity in conversations and reflections. Try to take the 'helicopter' view, whereby you can fly above the present and look down on what is happening. This can help to identify next steps or at least encourage further information gathering. Deliberately converse with others, be that other SENCOs or SEN Practitioners, or other staff and leaders in the setting as well as learners and their families. At times we may feel very alone in our roles, but we are not. Invest in deliberate conversations to explore thinking and to clarify ideas and actions. Reconnect with your values and allow these to inform the intent of your SEND leadership.

Dave Whitaker (2021), in his book *The Kindness Principle – Making Relational Behaviour Management in Schools*, reminds us of the importance of relationships and values. He writes:

> Your values, in a person-centred profession like education, should be your fundamental beliefs and therefore drive your behaviour. They should be the guiding principles that steer every relationship and interaction you have, whether that is with a colleague or a child. You are far more likely to be happy if you are successfully living out your values in your everyday life. It is not healthy to work in a system that doesn't align with your own values. Therefore, you must look after yourself as well as provide the best possible place for children to learn.
>
> *(page 13)*

Deliberately look after yourself! This is really important and at times so very difficult to do. Ensure that you have a break from the thinking, worrying, uncertainty and stress of it all. Engage in all or some of the mindfulness techniques that we promote with our learners and families. Remind yourself of your strengths and achievements, and, yes, I really am encouraging you to notice your successes every day! This will help, but it needs to be deliberate because at the time when it is most required, it will feel the least useful thing to do. If these steps do not feel sufficient, then seek advice and support as your health and wellbeing is the most important attribute. Deliberately promote mental health protective characteristics for yourself, whatever they look like for you. Deliberately engage with those things and people that make you smile, laugh and feel alive. Recharge yourself so can you continue to LEAD the SEND system.

Applying the SEND LEADership principles

The SEND LEADership Self-Evaluation contains a table of questions that are intended to encourage thinking and reflections on your application of these four LEADership principles. When time allows take a look and explore your strengths and areas for development with language, empowerment, ambition and deliberateness. Consider the strengths and areas for development of the SEND system as a whole, and also for you as an individual SENCO or SEN Practitioner. As always, there are no right or wrongs, but the process of reflection is intended to support you to 'check in' with yourself and your LEADership.

SEND LEADership Self-Evaluation

Language	Empowerment
Is there a consistency within the language used to describe learners with SEN, SEND and those with medical needs?	As leaders do we seek to empower all staff, governors, learners and families?
Do all staff share the importance of language choices?	Do our systems empower us and those around us?
Are our values towards language evidenced in policies and documents?	Do SEND approaches seek to build capacity of learners and encourage self-direction and ownership?
Is there a positive culture of challenge and support?	Do adults empower learners with SEND through the promotion of mediation and independent skills?
Do we make explicit the implicit with regards to our expectations and preferences for language use on an annual basis?	Are families able to participate and contribute to our development?
Ambition	**Deliberateness**
In what ways can we evidence-base our ambition for all learners, including those with SEND?	Is SEND leadership deliberate with clear intent, effective systems for implementation and measurable means of impact?
Do we promote self-ambition and belief in learners?	How do leaders of SEND promote the development and ownership of our vision for SEND systems?
Are families encouraged to be ambitious about learners and our school community?	Are we proactive and deliberate with our actions with intent?
Are we ambitious in our intent and implementation of SEND systems?	Are we deliberately enhancing the lived experience of learners with SEND in our setting?
Is this ambition evident in the impact of SEND systems on learner outcomes?	Are we deliberate in SEND assessment, planning, delivery and review to ensure the best outcomes for learners?

SEND LEADership – *Reflective Comments*

Our strengths …

Language	Empowerment
Ambition	**Deliberateness**

Our areas for development …

Language	Empowerment
Ambition	**Deliberateness**

My strengths as a SENCO …

Language	Empowerment
Ambition	Deliberateness

My areas for development as a SENCO …

Language	Empowerment

Ambition	Deliberateness

Reflections

- Do the four principles of SEND LEADership resonate for you?
- How consistent is language within the culture of your setting?
- Does the SEND system seek to empower, and is there evidence of ambition and deliberateness?

Actions to consider

- Rank the four LEADership principles in order of current effectiveness. Would other leaders and staff have the same view? Could you ask them?
- Facilitate a values conversation between staff and leaders, identifying shared values regarding teaching and learning. Are these values inclusive for all learners, including those with SEND?
- Plan an activity that will boost your well-being and bring you joy.

10. Getting started

So here we are at Chapter 10, which, in fact, is Chapter 30 within the Essential SENCO Toolkit as a whole, so well done us! Thank you for getting this far and continuing on our shared journey. Although the chapter is called "Getting Started", you are of course well and truly on your way. The reality of our roles is that they don't actually 'stop' or re-start. We do of course enjoy the 'pause' of school holidays, but even then our thinking and planning continues. However, the intention of the Essential SENCO Toolkit has been to offer you ideas and possible starting points in relation to SEND assessment, SEND intervention and SEND leadership, and this chapter is an opportunity to identify what resonates with you?

The purpose of this chapter is to interleave some of our key ideas to encourage reflection and refinement of possible actions. Every reader of the Essential SENCO Toolkit will adopt or adapt an idea individually in order to implement this in their own setting and the wonderful thing about writing a trilogy of strengths-based, practical and inclusive books is the opportunity to practice what is preached! The values underpinning the Essential SENCO Toolkit include a belief in your uniqueness and your capacity. They are embedded in a belief that what we give attention to becomes our reality. And the language that we use contributes to our reality. The entire toolkit is offered as a starting point, in full knowledge and acceptance of change, both in terms of the changes that you will make to the ideas and the expected changes to our national and local contexts. The offer of ideas and support really have been made authentically and have emerged from work with real children, families, SENCOs and staff. The Essential SENCO Toolkit is written with a belief that you are the storyteller of your own story. The delight and privilege that I feel when I hear an extract from your story is my motivation and reward as a writer. And I hugely believe that the ideas in the Essential SENCO Toolkit will build upon what you know and experience and empower you to dream for the future. I also believe in 'us' as a profession and our potential for collaborative capacity building, adaptation, and that we value and celebrate difference. Thus, illustrating how the Essential SENCO Toolkit has been written on a foundation of a strengths-based approach as described by Hammond (2010).

DOI: 10.4324/9781003408994-11

Embedding a strengths-based approach could be one of the themes that you adopt as your starting point or indeed next step? Introducing the 7 Cs Learning Porfolio could empower staff, learners and their families to adopt and adapt a shared language of strengths and areas for development. You may choose to start with the 4 Functions of Learning Support and promote greater clarity regarding the purposeful deployment of TAs. Utilising the ABC-D framework of targeted outcomes with staff could feel more of an immediate priority, or indeed establishing your own SEND Portfolio of Evidence? You may decide to use the annual strategic planner and the SEND QA Toolkit to help plan and gather information as part of your review of SEND in your setting. Or you may choose to work with other colleagues to engage with an SEND review audit, identifying the strengths and areas for development within the system. A focus for you could be reviewing the intent of your SEND system and the anticipated impact of your action with intent. Or it may involve a review of the consistency and shared understanding of all regarding the language of SEN, SEND and medical needs. The 7 Cs, 7 Ps and 7 Ds of leadership may have inspired an action for you, or the combined emphasis of CPD may prompt an evaluation of the development opportunities available both to staff and for yourself. By focusing on SEND LEADership and the quality assurance of intent, implementation and impact of SEND systems this may trigger an action plan or next step for you. Trust yourself and follow your professional interests. The extracts below include examples from four Trust leads and one local authority who have done exactly that. They are included as illustrations of possible applications of the Essential SENCO Toolkit and may aid your decision-making.

Diocese of Norwich Education and Academies Trust (DNEAT)

Rachael Judd – Academies Group Executive Principal (AGEP)

In collaboration with Judith Carter, I have led on the Trust's SEND priority for the last three years. This has been an absolute privilege. I have learned so much from Judith and gained great professional satisfaction from being part of a strengths-based leadership system.

The systems and processes that we now have in place across the Trust are the key infrastructure for our provision for pupils with SEND. We started with the Portfolio of Evidence which standardised how we would categorise and monitor the information about our SEND provision across each school. SEND Peer Reviews have provided us with a wholly collaborative and supportive way to provide challenge to our schools, whilst working with leaders to identify key priorities together. We have trained and utilised the skills of our learning centred leaders for SEND across the Trust who lead on the reviews. A strong quality assurance system provided by the AGEPs provides the important checks and balances that challenge the systems in place and checks their effectiveness and impact.

We also introduced the 7 Cs. This common language of assessment has been a focus for each school and practitioner and is now embedded. It has allowed us to reflect, evaluate and consider carefully on how each child with SEND is progressing by looking at their strengths and developments. It has also provided us with a common, easily accessible language that is supportive of the child, their parents and professionals.

As a result of the SEND priority, there are key systems in place that are embedded. These not only provide a systemised structure that supports and improves the provision for pupils with SEND, it also, by providing a common language, and ways of working, supports our children and their parents and of course ensures high quality provision for all".

Suffolk Local Authority

Claire Darwin – Principal Educational Psychologist

Suffolk County Council Inclusion Services started working with Judith Carter and using the Essential SENCO Toolkit in 2021. This person-centred, relational and strengths-based approach to assessment and intervention complemented a genuine endeavour to support schools and families by offering an approach that aligns with the aforementioned person-centred values. In summary, an approach that enables children and young people to be placed at the centre of planning next steps and support. The benefits of embedding this as part of the SEND Graduated Response in Suffolk has been to introduce a shared language for everyone across schools, for example, SENCOs, teaching assistants, teachers, children, young people and families, by providing a positive framework of discussion around recognising strengths, identifying additional needs, shaping and delivering interventions whilst also noting and celebrating the progress made by children and young people.

We all soon witnessed the benefits of offering the Essential SENCO Toolkit as part of Suffolks' offer with Judith's wonderfully knowledgeable, down to earth training style and wealth of practical experience. School and local authority (LA) staff were keen to embed and support this approach further as part of the LA offer. Empowering practice development sessions facilitated by Judith have also supported embedding the approach and creative use of the resources into everyday practice across schools. Staff feedback indicates that they have particularly valued the applicability of resources and ease of use. For example, by taking ideas and practice examples from the accompanying resources and using them to enhance and transform practice across their settings with tangible benefits being seen for children, young people and families.

As part of our LA resource we have also invested in a Suffolk Inclusion Toolkit Project Officer who is busy working with colleagues in the LA and school staff, including seeking feedback from families in order to capture impact over time. We have started to collate feedback that indicates the approach and resources have supported capacity building amongst staff and a greater sense of empowerment. It is also powerful to have the child or young person's voice at the centre of planning. As we continue to strengthen our implementation of this approach at a systemic level, we remain grateful for Judith's input and the practical resources within the Essential SENCO Toolkit that have helped so many to reflect and consider the theories that underpin the approach and translate this into evidence-informed practice.

Academy Transformation Trust (ATT)

Abigail Joachim – Institute Specialist

Academy Transformation Trust (ATT) is a cross-phase group of 21 academies, including primary, secondary, post-16 and further education settings, operating across ten English local authority areas. In 2022, we welcomed a new CEO, Sir Nick Weller, and have recently undergone significant restructuring around the central team, with particular focus on safeguarding and SEND.

Our mission as a Trust is to 'transform life chances by achieving the highest possible standards and preparing all our students to lead successful lives' and a key strategic priority to achieve this is through aligned autonomy. As a newly formed Trust Inclusion Team, this meant researching the market to find a common framework to provide a shared approach with the flexibility for this to be applied in a context specific way, at academy level. We were fortunate to be introduced to the benefits of the Essential SENCO Toolkit through our Suffolk-based academies when their local authority adopted it as part of their graduated response. It was clear that this strengths-based framework aligned with our vision for adaptive practice, teaching assistant deployment and intervention and offered a common language of assessment.

As a geographically spread Trust, effective, routine and regular partnership and collaboration across our academies is essential and is facilitated through a structure of professional communities. The SEND community provides an opportunity for our SENDCos to collectively engage in discussion and practice sharing, which offered the perfect platform to begin launching the new framework. Ensuring that our SEND leaders receive detailed training in all aspects of the Essential SENCO Toolkit, has been the foundation to the implementation process, which has begun with a focus on the language of the 7 Cs and how this can enhance our universal provision. Through our Adaptive Teaching Twilight series, colleagues across the Trust also started to explore the framework, examining teacher tweaks and TA deployment in the classroom, which culminated in a Trust-wide PD day considering role-specific application of the 7 Cs. Although early in our journey as a Trust, each of our academies is approaching the framework in relation to their individual starting points and are at various stages of the implementation cycle.

At Ravens Academy in Clacton, their newly appointed SENDCo is excited to begin exploring the framework with their staff team. Having recently completed the Maximising the Practice of Teaching Assistants training, focused on evidence-informed strategies to develop pupil independence, the Essential SENCO Toolkit provides a perfect next step.

Preparation for implementation at Iceni Secondary in Thetford, has involved incorporating the language of the 7 Cs within existing one-page profiles and adaptive practice sheets. Their staged approach to facilitating effective adaptive teaching begins with the clear strategies outlined on the one-page profiles of pupils on the SEND register. These are then transferred to class-specific adaptive practice sheets, highlighting common strategies that relate to a range of pupils within the group. These common strategies are then summarised into a set of key class strategies, which will not only meet the needs of pupils with SEND but will also create a more inclusive environment for all.

As one of our Suffolk-based academies, Great Heath in Mildenhall has had a little longer to engage with the framework and is beginning to deliver aspects within their primary setting. Initially, this involved whole staff training to ensure the language of the 7 Cs was well understood and could be accurately employed to identify strengths and areas for development. This has facilitated the formation of targeted outcomes to overcome, reduce or remove barriers to learning, and has led to improvements to their universal offer. The next steps for Great Heath are to hone targeted outcomes to ensure they are specific and measurable, and to develop the role of teaching assistants via the four functions of learning support.

At Caldmore Primary in Walsall, the framework already aligns with the inclusive practices embedded throughout their academy. They operate under the mantra that 'good practice for pupils with SEND is good practice for all', incorporating adaptive strategies, such as visuals, concrete resources and now and next boards into their universal provision. Their focus on vocabulary building and language development, through approaches like 'Word Aware' and 'Colourful Semantics', and the role their teaching assistants take in supporting learning via mediation in the classroom, match the principles underpinning the Essential SENCO Toolkit. At Caldmore, they are now at the stage of sustaining their inclusive culture, interweaving the framework to embed the language of the 7 Cs and the four functions of learning support into their everyday practices.

While these short case studies only offer snapshots, representing examples of how academies across ATT are engaging with the framework at different stages of implementation, they demonstrate the importance of the aligned autonomy that is at the heart of our Trust. The common threads, including a shared language of assessment, strategies to overcome and remove barriers to learning and a clear TA deployment model, will become part of our aligned approach, but our academies will retain the autonomy to apply these depending on their individual contexts.

The Wensum Trust

Dr Rachel Wilson – Educational Psychologist

We have used Judith's *SEND Assessment* and *SEND Intervention* Essential SENCo Toolkit to evaluate and entirely re-work the approach we take to SEND across our Trust of 11 schools. Each school has benefited from a renewed focus on children's strengths and from having a shared language to use to explore barriers to learning and inform planning to overcome and remove these. Our Trust SENDCos work as a team and this shared approach and shared language has facilitated that team work and made a real difference for our children and families. Judith's 7 Cs approach is now well embedded in our schools and we plan to continue to build from this, trying out more and more of the tools on offer.

St Benet's Multi-Academy Trust

Nadine Avenal – Trust Improvement Lead for SEND

Case study

St Benet's is a growing Multi-Academy Trust providing education for children and young people in Norfolk and the Waveney Valley. Some academies are very small and rural; others are much larger and are in market towns. Each academy has their own distinctive character, but all operate within the Christian ethos and values of the of Norwich and St Benet's Multi-Academy Trust. The MAT has a higher number of pupils than the national average identified with SEND (around 20%).

In September 2023, the Trust introduced the 7 Cs materials to provide a shared language of SEND across the Trust and to support the development of robust APDR plans which would contribute to improving pupils' outcomes. This was launched with a 7 Cs conference, which was attended by SENDCos, teachers, governors and central team members. Academies chose to explore the 7 Cs materials at either 'Interested Novice' or 'Experienced User' level with a follow-up session held during the Spring term, to review implementation and share good practice. By working collaboratively and using a shared framework of SEND support, Trust academies have begun reducing bureaucracy, increasing co-production with pupils and parents/carers, and empowering teachers to target SEND provision more effectively. In order to integrate the 7 Cs materials with other Trust resources and to align these to the evidence required to access the SEND top-up funding system in Norfolk, a number of bespoke resources were created, which include:

Learning portfolio

The 7 Cs Learning Portfolio was adapted into a simple, one-page baseline tool to support school staff with creating individual pupil profiles, whereby each of the 7 Cs elements can be considered and identified as possible strengths or barriers to learning. For many academies this is now used to inform the initial APDR cycle at the start of each year.

APDRs

The Trust's model APDR format was adapted to incorporate the 7 Cs in a structured and meaningful way that would be accessible to pupils and parents/carers. Teachers are able to utilise the 7 Cs action cards and sample targeted outcomes resources to support them with completing these termly plans.

Personalised bookmarks/desk prompts

Feedback from quality assurance activities revealed that although APDR plans were being created and shared with pupils, they were not always able to recall the provision that was in place to support them or articulate their targets. In order to strengthen the pupils' knowledge and understanding of support, academies created a personalised bookmark or desk prompt to capture the pupils' termly targeted outcomes and visual 'self-help' toolbox.

Progress analysis

Once academies had begun using the 7 Cs tracker, the Trust created a spreadsheet to capture 7 Cs focus elements and pupils' progress in a comparative way. This has enabled a more strategic use of the 7 Cs data at both an individual academy and Trust level. Leaders can use this data to reflect on key questions such as:

- What are the most common 7 Cs Elements being focused on?
- How can CPD and school resources be used to support these focus areas?
- Are there any class/year group/academy trends?
- Is provision being used to target the most significant barriers to learning?
- Are pupils making expected progress?

Initial feedback from the introduction of the 7 Cs materials has been incredibly positive, with school staff reporting that they feel well supported by the wealth of resources available to assist them in identifying pupils' barriers to learning and to aid them with creating more focused APDR plans. Pupil and parent/carer co-production has also increased, which can certainly be attributed, at least in part, to the more accessible language of the 7 Cs Learning Portfolio and supporting materials for families. This shared language of SEND support and the clear structure for capturing the *'different from or additional to'* provision, has also been of great benefit to Senior Leaders, Governors and Trustees, who now have a common framework to use when reflecting on SEND provision and outcomes at a strategic level. Ultimately though, the 7 Cs materials have allowed our academies to take a more holistic view of each child and personalise their SEND provision, so that the right support can be given at the right time.

	Pupil			Class		
	Completed by			Date		

7 Cs LEARNING PORTFOLIO©
Assessment of Strengths & Barriers to Learning

	Element	Significant Difficulty	Difficulty	Neutral	Strength	Significant Strength		Element	Significant Difficulty	Difficulty	Neutral	Strength	Significant Strength
COGNITION	Working Memory Capacity to hold and manipulate information						**COMMUNICATION**	Expressive Vocabulary Subject and category words					
	Speed of Processing Time taken to assimilate information							Articulation Accuracy of pronunciation					
	Inference Using information to make predictions							Language & Comprehension Understanding of spoken language					
	Anticipation Pause, consider & identify possible outcomes							Collaborative Conversation Turn taking & responding to questions					
	Reflection Noticing actions and impact							Listening Extracting information from speech					
	Evaluation Weighing up and making judgements							Social Communication (Output) Use of verbal & non-verbal communication					
	Analysis Combining information							Social Interaction (Input) Reaction to verbal & non-verbal cues					
CREATIVITY	Generation of Ideas Thoughts and ideas						**CONTROL**	Self-Regulation Control & manage behaviour, emotions & language					
	Problem Solving Using initiative to find solutions (includes gaming)							Behaviour for Learning Readiness to engage & participate					
	Attention Sustained focus an concentration							Anxiety Management Control over fear and anxious thoughts					
	Motivation Eager and willing to engage							Confidence Belief in self and own capacity to contribute					
	Making Things Designing, constructing, craft							Resilience Capacity to 'bounce back' and try again					
	Courage & Determination Fearless to have a go and sustain effort							Language of Emotions Ability to label feelings					
	Trust Secure in self and those around them							Independence Capacity to work alone					
COMPASSION	Friendships Initiate & sustain positive relationships with peers						**CO-ORDINATION**	Fine Motor Handwriting, cut, thread, manipulation with fingers					
	Turn Taking Ability to wait, follow rules and share							Gross Motor Run, walk, jump, skip, kick, catch & throw					
	Empathy To anticipate experiences of others							Sensory Vision, hearing & tracking					
	Sense of Justice Own ethical code and sense of right & wrong							Mobility Independent movement					
	Self-Esteem & Well being Sense of self-worth and value of self-care							Stability & Balance Control over movement					
	Self-Efficacy Belief in own capacity to effect change							Posture Effective positioning					
	Support for Others Befriend and encourage others							Sensory Processing Filter, respond or extract sensory information					
CURRICULUM	English Reading, writing & spelling							**Other:**					
	Maths Number, money, time, shape, space							**3 KEY STRENGTHS (From these elements)**					
	Science Biology, chemistry & physics							1. 2. 3.					
	Creative Arts Art, music, drama & dance												
	Humanities History, Geography & Religious Education							**3 INITIAL FOCUS AREAS (From these elements)**					
	ICT Computing & gaming							1. 2. 3.					
	PE & Sports Games, athletics, gymnastics & sports												

Copyright material from Judith Carter (2025), *SEND Leadership*, Routledge

Autumn Term Targets

This term we are focusing on these 3 elements:

	Baseline (Assess) - What can they do now?	Targeted Outcome - What will success look like?	Outcome (Review) - How did they get on?	7 Cs Tracker
1				Baseline Outcome Progress
2				Baseline Outcome Progress
3				Baseline Outcome Progress

Provision (Plan & Do)

To help develop these skills in school we will:	Interventions *(If applicable)*

At home or when you are out and about you should:

My Self-Help Toolbox
Things I will do or use to help myself succeed

Provision Review

	👍 What's going well / What's working?	👎 What's not going well / What's not working?
Pupil Voice		
Teacher Voice		
Parent / Carer Voice		
Important dates or updates since last review meeting		
What will we change?		
Focus elements agreed for Spring		

Name: Pupil Example My Autumn Term 7 Cs Focus Areas		
Working Memory	Listening	Resilience
I will remember 3 parts of an instruction so I can follow **multi**-step **instructions** in school and at home.	I will **identify the key information** needed to complete a task, and tell my buddy, to demonstrate my **effective listening skills**.	I will **identify 3 positive** achievements each week to be recorded in my WOW book so I can start to reflect on my successes and strengths.

My Self-Help Toolbox

Break things down into steps or stages	Check list	Highlighter pens	Post-it notes	Wow book	Self-belief – I know I can do this!

Name:

My Spring Term 7 Cs Focus Areas

Element 1	Element 2	Element 3

My Self-Help Toolbox

Name:

My Summer Term 7 Cs Focus Areas

Element 1	Element 2	Element 3

My Self-Help Toolbox

Copyright material from Judith Carter (2025), *SEND Leadership*, Routledge

Example Primary Academy
Diocese of Norwich — St Benet's Multi Academy Trust
7 Cs Tracker© Overview & Analysis

Willow Tree Learning

Year Group		Alice	Betty	Chris	Dave	Eddie	Fred	Greg	Henry	Ian	Name	Name	Name	Name	Name	Name	Name	Name
		4	N	N	5	6	2	2	R	3								
Autumn	Focus 1	Communication	Communication	Communication	Control	Curriculum	Cognition	Communication	Coordination	Creativity								
		Expressive Vocabulary	Articulation	Articulation	Self-Regulation	English	Working Memory	Social Communication	Fine Motor	Trust								
	Tracker Sept	2	2	2	2	3	3	2	4	2								
	Tracker Dec	4	2	3	1	3	4	4	4	6								
	Progress	2	0	1	-1	0	1	2	3	4								
	Focus 2	Communication	Compassion	Cognition	Compassion	Cognition	Cognition	Cognition	Creativity	Control								
		Collaborative Conversation	Self-Esteem & Well being	Speed of Processing	Empathy	Inference	Speed of Processing	Working Memory	Attention	Behaviour for Learning								
	Tracker Sept	2	4	3	1	3	3	3	2	2								
	Tracker Dec	3	5	3	3	4	4	4	1	2								
	Progress	1	1	0	2	1	1	1	-1	0								
	Focus 3	Cognition	Coordination	Communication	Cognition	Cognition	Curriculum	Cognition	Control	Communication								
		Reflection	Sensory	Listening	Working Memory	Anticipation	English	Speed of Processing	Behaviour for Learning	Social Interaction								
	Tracker Sept	3	4	2	4	3	2	2	3	2								
	Tracker Dec	4	5	2	5	4	2	2	4	3								
	Progress	1	1	0	1	2	0	0	1	1								
Spring	Focus 1																	
	Tracker Jan																	
	Tracker March																	
	Progress																	
	Focus 2																	
	Tracker Jan																	
	Tracker March																	
	Progress																	
	Focus 3																	
	Tracker Jan																	
	Tracker March																	
	Progress																	
Summer	Focus 1																	
	Tracker April																	
	Tracker July																	
	Progress																	
	Focus 2																	
	Tracker April																	
	Tracker July																	
	Progress																	
	Focus 3																	
	Tracker April																	
	Tracker July																	
	Progress																	
Total Points Progress		4	2	1	2	3	2	3	3	5	0	0	0	0	0	0	0	0

Copyright material from Judith Carter (2025), *SEND Leadership*, Routledge

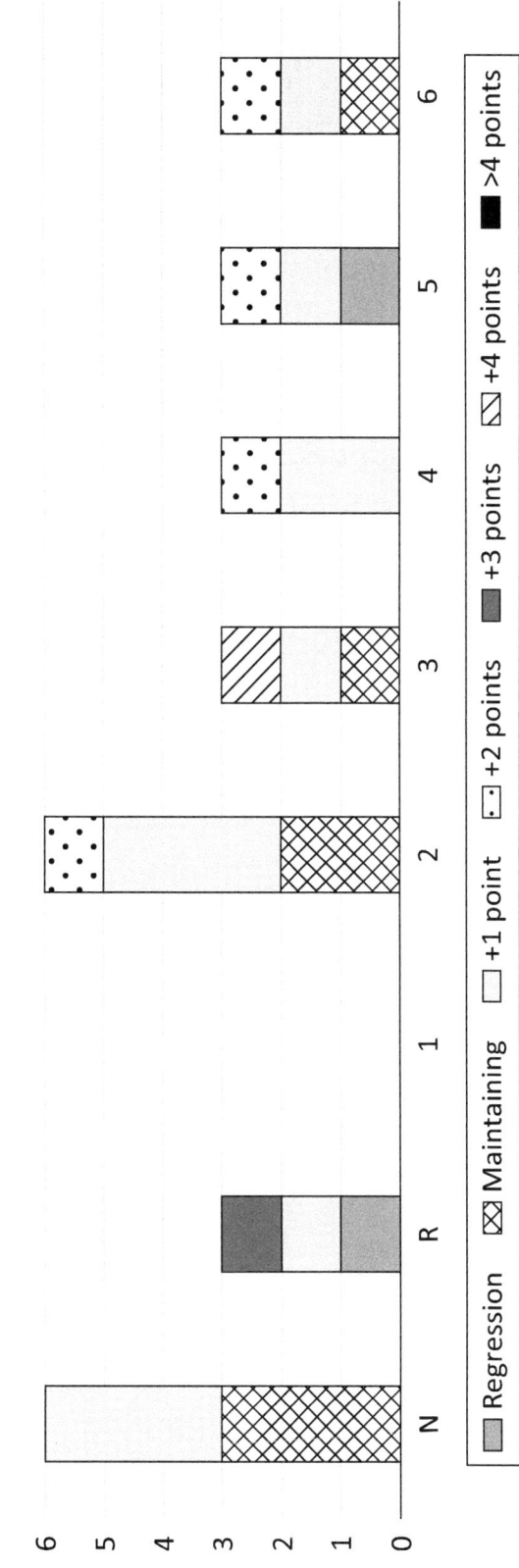

Personalised next steps

The inclusion of these case studies and the contributions from individual SENCOs and SEN Practitioners integrated throughout the book, are intended to support you as you plan your first or next steps. A Professionals Action Planning Tool is included here to encourage your reflection and to aid your planning. There is a growing network of expertise and experience regarding the implementation of the Essential SENCO Toolkit so please do talk to colleagues, ask questions and maximise our opportunities for collaboration. Additional information can be accessed via my website www.willowtreelearning.co.uk and please share a comment or post a question to me directly by email to Judith.carter@willowtreelearning.co.uk. Download the resources from Routledge Speechmark and adopt or adapt to suit your priorities. Reflect on your leadership strengths and areas for development and continue to strive towards clarity and consistency of SEND intent, implementation and impact.

SEND Leadership – Professionals Action Planning Tool

What I liked about the book:

What resonated the most with me at this time was:

What I would like to do as a result of reading this book:

How could I achieve this?

What barriers may I face?

How can I 'overcome' or 'remove' these barriers?

Who would be interested in working with me on this?

What do I need to do first?

Core attributes of the Essential SENCO Toolkit

The effective implementation of the Essential SENCO Toolkit will be different for everyone. It is designed that way. It is a flexible, strengths-based approach intended to support you in your role. That said, there are core attributes that are intended to guide you in your use of the materials. The approach should be:

- **Strengths-based** and promote individual uniqueness and capacity
- **Consistent** with a shared understanding of language and intent
- **Creative** yet evidence-based
- **Practical** and informed by starting points
- **Purposeful** and add value to your role and the lived experience of staff, learners and their families
- **Measurable** – intent informs implementation which enables the identification of impact
- **Supportive**, positive and encouraging
- **Dynamic**, flexible and adaptive
- **Empowering** to all
- **Ambitious**, leading to good outcomes

As you implement the Essential SENCO toolkit, you may find yourself utilising the learning attributes of the 7 Cs from your own learning profile! You will after all apply your **cognitive** skills as you think about intent, implementation and impact. You will maximise your skills of **communication** as you gather and share information with others. You will adopt and or adapt the approaches in a **creative** manner, sustaining **control** and **compassion** as you **co-ordinate** the dissemination of this **'curriculum'** or approach. So, it appears, the 7 Cs, really are the starting and finishing point of the Essential SENCO toolkit, and our journey together!

Our final shared words, however, are taken from Dave Whitaker's book *The Kindness Principle* and have been chosen as a reminder of what we already know. You know so much, and you have all the skills, capacity and energy (believe it or not,) to continue to make a difference for children and young people with SEND. So, thank you for all you do to support learners with SEND, and for all you will continue to do. I hope the Essential SENCO Toolkit helps you to **live what you believe** …

We know that great schools do not need to show an Ofsted outstanding banner on the front gate. Wonderful schools open their doors to visitors and there is pride and warmth in every corridor and classroom. Staff and children are happy, and the community is thriving. Unconditional positive regard is tangible in every interaction. Great schools do not need a badge of honour; **they live what they believe,** and this is what makes them truly outstanding.

(Whitaker, 2021, page 12)

Thank you and good wishes.

References

Cambridge English Dictionary (2024) 'Dynamic.' Available at https://dictionary.cambridge.org/dictionary/english/dynamic

Code of Practice on the Identification and Assessment of Special Educational Needs (1994) – Department for Education

Collins Dictionary (2024) 'Impact.' Available at https://www.collinsdictionary.com/dictionary/english/impact

Continuing Professional Development and Your Registration (2024) Health Care Professionals Council.

How to Lead for Daring New Leaders: The No-Nonsense Guide to Develop Basic Leadership Skills (2022) Paul A Wyatt.

Index for Inclusion: Developing Learning and Participation in Schools (2011) Tony Booth and Mel Ainscow. Bristol: Centre for Studies in Inclusive Education (CSIE).

Independent Review of Teachers' Professional Development in Schools: Phase 1 Findings. (2024) 'Ofsted.' Available at https://www.gov.uk/government/publications/teachers-professional-development-in-schools/independent-review-of-teachers-professional-development-in-schools-phase-1-findings

Independent Review of Teachers' Professional Development in Schools: Phase 2 Findings (2024) 'Ofsted.' Available at https://www.gov.uk/government/publications/teachers-professional-development-in-schools/independent-review-of-teachers-professional-development-in-schools-phase-2-findings

PositivePsychology.com (2024) 'Strengths-Based Practice.' Available at https://positivepsychology.com/strengths-based-interventions/

Principles of Strengths-based Practice (2010) Wayne Hammond. Resiliency Initiatives. Available at https://www.cycaa.com/wp-content/uploads/2020/07/PrinciplesOfStrength-BasedPractice.pdf

SEND Assessment: A Strengths-based Framework for Learners with SEND (2021) Judith Carter Routledge.

SEND Intervention: Planning Provision with Purpose (2022) Judith Carter Routledge.

She Thinks Like a Boss: Leadership – 9 Essential Skills for New Female Leaders in Business and the Workplace (2021) Jemma Roedel.

Special Educational Needs and Disability Code of Practice: 0-25 years – Statutory Guidance for Organisations with Work with and Support Children and Young

People Who Have Special Educational Needs or Disabilities (2014; updated 2015) Department for Education.

Standard for Teachers Professional Development (2016) Department for Education.

Supporting Pupils with Medical Needs in School - Statutory Guidance about the Support That Pupils with Medical Conditions Should Receive at School Department for Education (2014) Available at https://www.gov.uk/government/publications/supporting-pupils-at-school-with-medical-conditions--3

Teacher Standards Department for Education (2021) Available at https://assets.publishing.service.gov.uk/media/5a750668ed915d3c7d529cad/Teachers_standard_information.pdf

The CPD Curriculum – Creating Conditions for Growth (2021) Zoe Enser and Mark Enser. Crown House Publishing.

The Dynamic Assessment of Retarded Performers: The Learning Potential Assessment Device, Theory, Instruments and Techniques (1979) Feuerstein, Rand & Hoffman. University Park Press.

The Education Endowment Foundation – Blog by Jon Eaton – Moving from Differentiation to Adaptive Teaching. Available at https://www.gov.uk/government/publications/supporting-pupils-at-school-with-medical-conditions--3

The Education Endowment Foundation – Making Best Use of Teaching Assistants. Available at https://educationendowmentfoundation.org.uk/education-evidence/guidance-reports/teaching-assistants

The Education Endowment Foundation – Effective Professional Development. Available at https://educationendowmentfoundation.org.uk/education-evidence/guidance-reports/effective-professional-development

The Kindness Principle: Making Relational Behaviour Management Work in Schools (2021) Dave Whitaker.

Twinkl (2023) Available at https://www.twinkl.co.uk/teaching-wiki/qulaity-assurance

Index

4 Functions of Learning Support 31, 157–159
7 Cs Learning Portfolio 9, 11, 90; intent of 88–89; Progress Tracker 175–176; quality assurance (QA) 176–177
7 Ds of leadership 18–20; daring leadership 21; deliberate leadership 20; developmental leadership 23–24; distributed leadership 24–25; doable leadership 22–23; dutiful leadership 22; dynamic leadership 20–21; *see also* SEND LEADership

A4 booklet 9
ABC-D scaffold for targeted outcomes 140–146, 160
academy action plan, SEND review audit 128–133
Academy Transformation Trust (ATT) 215–217
achievement 78–79, 137
action planning 127
"action with intent" 8; SEND provisions 79
adapted curriculum 6
Adapted Teaching A-Z prompt booklet 11–16
adaptive teaching 89–90
adjustments 92–94; *see also* adaptive teaching
adoption of strengths-based approach 177–179
ADPRs, St Benet's Multi-Academy Trust 218
AEI *see* SEND Audit evidence ideas
ambition, SEND LEADership 203
annual strategic plans, protecting time with an annual strategic planner 50–59
anticipated intent 70
APDR Analysis 46
ATT *see* Academy Transformation Trust
attainment: curriculum attainment 137; and intent 78–79; personalised attainment 137
Audit Evaluation Prompt (AEP) 97–99
Audit Evidence Ideas (AEI) 100–102
Avenal, Nadine 218–219

best endeavours, Code of Practice 2015 21

case sampling 146–151; quality assurance activity 147–151
Children and Families Act 2014 5
Code of Practice 1994 180
Code of Practice 2015 5, 21, 71; quality assurance (QA) 29–30; SEN Information Report 30
collaboration 60
compliance in SEN Information Report 74–75
Continued Professional Development (CPD) 185–187, 199
curriculum attainment 137

daring leadership 21
Darwin, Claire 214–215
deliberate leadership 20
deliberateness, SEND LEADership 203–205
describing learners 8
desk prompts 219
developmental leadership 23–24
differentiation 91
Diocese of Norwich Education and Academies Trust (DNEAT) 94, 111, 213–214
distributed leadership 24–25
DNEAT *see* Diocese of Norwich Education and Academies Trust
doable leadership 22–23
dutiful leadership 22
dynamic leadership 20–21

Early Careers Teachers (ECTs) 186
Education Endowment Foundation 158, 185
Education, Health and Care Plan (EHCP) 78, 84, 90; implementation of 180–183
empowerment, SEND LEADership 202–203
Equality Act 2010 5, 92
Essential SENCO Toolkit 212; core attributes of 228–229
evaluating: purpose 189; SEND systems 60–61; from a learner's perspective 180

Index

Family Consultation – Interview Schedule 39
Family Questionnaire 43
feedback 60–67

identifying: learners with SEN 5–6; starting point for the use of 4 Functions of Learning Support 157–159
impact 136; case sampling 146–151; learner perspective form 151–153; targeted outcomes 140; triangulated impact 136–139
implementation of SEND 90–91; action planning 127; adaptive teaching 91–92; adjustments 92–94; SEND Audit evidence ideas (AEI) 100–102; SEND Portfolio of Evidence 94–99; SEND review audit letter with timetable 113; SEND review audit tool 111–112
implementation of EHCPs 180–183
inferred strengths, weaknesses, opportunities and threats 134
intent 8, 68–70, 75; and attainment 78–79; defining 79; SEN Information Report 71–72; SEND Development Plan 79–83; SEND Intent Self-Evaluation 75–77
interviews, quality assurance (QA) 31
introducing language of 7 Cs to staff, learners and families 155–157
involvement of others 60

Joachim, Abigail 215–217
Judd, Rachael 213–214

language: importance of 8; SEND LEADership 201–202; *see also* shared language
leadership *see also* 7 Ds of leadership, SEND LEADership
Leadership Self-Evaluation form 25–28
Learner Engagement Observation Schedule 37
Learner Evaluation – Interview Schedule 38
learner ownership 31
learner participation, promoting with 7 Cs 160–174
learner perspective form 151–153
Learner Questionnaire 42
learners: describing 8; groups of 5; with learning difficulty that requires special educational provision 5; with medical needs 5; with physical and/or mental impairment 5

learning support walk 30–31, 35; observation prompts 120

MARI *see* mediation, assessment, reinforcement and intervention
mediated learning experience (MLE) 68–69, 157
mediation 68
mediation, assessment, reinforcement and intervention (MARI) 159
MLE *see* mediated learning experience
My CPD Record 197–198
My Learning Plan 163–174
My SEND CPD Summary Record 192

observation prompts, learning support walk 120

paperwork, purpose of 70
personalised attainment 137
personalised bookmarks/desk prompts 219
picnic lunch box anaology 6, 91–92
planners, protecting time with 50–59
practical management 154; adoption of strengths-based approach 177–179; evaluating SEND system from a learner's perspective 180; identifying starting point for the use of 4 Functions of Learning Support 157–159; implementation of EHCPs 180–183; introducing language of 7 Cs to staff, learners and families 155–157; promoting learner participation 160–174; setting up SEND Portfolio of Evidence 179; supporting staff by writing relevant targeted outcomes 159–160; using 7 Cs Progress Tracker 175–176
Professional Evaluation – Termly Notes to Self 55, 59
progress analysis, St Benet's Multi-Academy Trust 218–226
Progress Tracker 175–176
promoting learner participation 160–174
protecting time with an annual strategic planner 50–59
purpose, evaluating 189

quality assurance (QA) 29–30; case sampling 147–150; creating a task list 47–49; involving others 60; methodology 30–46; practical management 176–177; protecting time with

Index

an annual strategic planner 50–59; regularly feeding back 60–67
question prompts, triangulated SEND review audit 117–119
questionnaires: Family Questionnaire 43; Learner Questionnaire 42; quality assurance (QA) 31; TA Questionnaire 45; Teacher Questionnaire 44

RAAG rating prompts 106–110
reasonable adjustments 92–94
recording sheet 115–116
reflective comments, SEND LEADership 207–210
regularly feeding back 60–67
review of professional development in schools 186–187

sandwich analogy 6, 8–9
SE *see* self-evaluation
Self Evaluation Summary Sheet 106–110
self-evaluation (SE): SEND LEADership 206; SEND Portfolio of Evidence 103–104
SEN Information Report 30, 36, 71–72; compliance with 72–74
SEN policy 71–72
SENCO Annual Strategic Plan 52–54, 56–58
SENCO QA Toolkit 30
SEND Audit Evaluation Prompt 94
SEND Audit evidence ideas (AEI) 100–101
SEND CPD Activity Planner – Willow Tree Primary Academy Annual Planner 194–195
SEND CPD Activity – School Planner 193
SEND Development Plan 81–83; example 84–87
SEND development plan Willow Tree Primary Academy (example) 84–87
SEND Intent Self-Evaluation 75–77
SEND LEADership 200–201; ambition 203; deliberateness 203–205; empowerment 202; language 201–202; reflective comments 207–208; self-evaluation (SE) 206
SEND Leadership – Professionals Action Planning Tool 227
SEND Portfolio of Evidence 94–96, 102; Audit Evaluation Prompt (AEP) 97–98; self-evaluation (SE) 103–105; self-evaluation, RAAG rating prompts 106–111; SEND review audit tool 111–112; setting up 179

SEND provisions 6, 79
SEND Quality Assurance Toolkit 32–34
SEND Report to Governors 61–63
SEND review audit, academy action plan 128–134
SEND review audit letter with timetable 113; triangulated SEND review audit letter with timetable 114
SEND review audit tool 111–112; recording sheet 115–116
SEND self-evaluation, RAAG rating prompts 106–111
SEND-themed CPD 196–199; activity planning tool 190–191; planning 191–199; staff audit 187–190
shared humanity 92
shared language 5, 156
SMART targets 140
St Benet's Multi-Academy Trust 218–219; 7 Cs Learning Portfolio 219; APDRs 219; personalised bookmarks/desk prompts 219; personalised next steps 226; progress analysis 219–220
Statement of Special Educational Needs 180–181
strengths, weaknesses, opportunities and threats (SWOT) 127; inferred strengths, weaknesses, opportunities and threats 134
strengths-based approach 177–179, 213
Suffolk Local Authority 214–215
supporting staff by writing relevant targeted outcomes 159–160

TA Evaluation – Interview Schedule, 41
TA Questionnaire, 42
targeted outcomes: ABC-D scaffold for targeted outcomes 140–146; and impact 140; supporting staff by writing relevant targeted outcomes 159–160
task lists, QA task lists 47–49
Teacher Evaluation – Interview Schedule 40
Teacher Questionnaire 42
Teacher Standards 186
teacher tweaks 92; *see also* adjustments
triangulated impact 136–139
triangulated SEND review audit letter with timetable 113
triangulated SEND review audits 127

Index

triangulated SEND review question prompts: questions for families 125; questions for governors 123; questions for learners 124; questions for SENCO 118–119; questions for TAs 122; questions for teachers 121; team meeting discussion prompt 126

The Wensum Trust 218

Will School SEN Report to Governors – Example 62–67

Wilson, Rachel 218

worksheets: 7 Cs Learning Portfolio 10; ABC-D scaffold for targeted outcomes 141; APDR Analysis 46; A-Z of Adaptive Teaching Practical Prompts 14–16; EHCP implementation plan 182–183; Family Consultation – Interview Schedule 39; Family Questionnaire 42; Inferred Strengths, Weaknesses, Opportunities and Threats 34; Leadership Self-Evaluation 26–27; Learner Engagement Observation Schedule 37; Learner Evaluation – Interview Schedule 38; Learner perspective form 152; Learner Questionnaire 42; Learning Support Walk 35; Mediation prompt process 69; My CPD Record 197–198; My Learning Plan 163–174; My SEND CPD Summary Record 192; Professional Evaluation – Termly Notes to Self 55, 59; Quality assurance activity: case sampling 147–150; Questions for families 125; Questions for Governors 123; Questions for learners 124; Questions for TAs 122; Questions for teachers 121; Recording sheet 115–116; SEN Information Report – Practical Application 36; SEN Profile – Who are our learners with SEN? 62–63; SENCO Annual Strategic Plan 52–54, 56–58; SEND Audit evidence ideas (AEI) 100–101; SEND CPD Activity Planner – Willow Tree Primary Academy Annual Planner 194–195; SEND CPD Activity Planning Tool 191; SEND CPD Activity – School Planner 193; SEND Development Plan 81–83; SEND Intent Self-Evaluation 76–77; SEND Leadership – Professionals Action Planning Tool 227; SEND LEADership – reflective comments 207–210; SEND LEADership self-evaluation 205; SEND Portfolio of Evidence Audit Evaluation Prompt (AEP) 97–98; SEND Portfolio of Evidence – self-evaluation 103–104; SEND Quality Assurance Toolkit 34; SEND Review Audit 128–133; SEND Self-Evaluation – RAAG Rating Prompts 106–110; SEND-themed CPD Staff Audit 188; TA Evaluation – Interview Schedule 41; TA Questionnaire 42; Teacher Evaluation – Interview Schedule 40; Teacher Questionnaire 42; Team meeting discussion prompt 126; Triangulated SEND Review Audit, question prompts 117–119

For Product Safety Concerns and Information please contact our EU representative GPSR@taylorandfrancis.com Taylor & Francis Verlag GmbH, Kaufingerstraße 24, 80331 München, Germany